CONTENTS

100 Years of Family-Made Goodness

JEROME M. SMUCKER

In honor of our centennial year, we at The J.M. Smucker Company have produced this collection of 100 recipes, all created to showcase the family-made goodness of Smucker's. Five of the recipes – one in each recipe category – were submitted by employees whose winning ways with Smucker's products earned them top honors in a Company-sponsored 100th anniversary recipe contest.

Jams, jellies and preserves have always been essential breakfast pleasures, but as these recipes attest, fruit spreads are too delicious to merely top toast. These recipes offer wonderful ideas for using fruit spreads to enliven food with flavor and color without adding fat, cholesterol, and calories. Culinary experts and novices alike will find an abundance of ideas for creating dazzling new appetizers, entrées, and desserts, as well as rediscovering some treasured old favorites.

CREAMY FRUIT BLINTZES RECIPE ON PAGE 94

People throughout the world enjoy fruit spreads on a variety of baked goods and as an enhancement to all kinds of dishes. The Smucker family and the more than 2,000 employees of The J.M. Smucker Company hope you enjoy these recipes.

The taste of Smucker's dates back to 1897, when in Orrville, Ohio, Jerome Smucker opened a small cider mill. He pressed apples harvested from his own trees and from neighboring farmers' orchards, many of which had been planted by Johnny Appleseed.

Word of the goodness of Jerome's products quickly spread, and soon he expanded his line to include apple butter made from his grandfather's Pennsylvania Dutch recipe. Jerome packaged his apple butter in clay crocks and hand-signed the paper lid on each, thus adding his personal guarantee and establishing the tradition of putting the Smucker name on only the highest-quality products.

Jerome's apple butter proved to be even more popular than his cider. Before long, his son Willard was selling half-gallon crocks of apple butter for 25 cents each from the back of a wagon he drove house to house.

The Smucker Story

By the 1920s, The J.M. Smucker Company offered a full complement of preserves, jams, and jellies. The company first shipped preserves and jellies from Orrville to Los Angeles in 1942, marking the beginning of national product distribution. Ice cream toppings and peanut butter were added to the growing list of Smucker's products.

In the century since Jerome Smucker's products were sold from the back of a horse-drawn wagon, The J.M. Smucker Company has grown to become the nation's largest producer of jams, jellies, preserves, ice cream toppings, natural peanut butter and fruit syrups.

Today, it is an international company with products found in more than 60 countries.

For four generations, the members of the Smucker family have been committed to creating quality products while adhering to Jerome Smucker's traditional values. And they still call Orrville, Ohio, home.

Measuring Smucker's Products

12-OUNCE JAR JELLY, JAM, PRESERVES, MARMALADE = 1 CUP

18-OUNCE JAR JELLY, JAM, PRESERVES, MARMALADE = $1\frac{1}{2}$ CUPS

32-OUNCE JAR JELLY, JAM = $2\frac{3}{4}$ CUPS

11-OUNCE JAR APPLE BUTTER = 1 CUP

16.5-OUNCE JAR APPLE BUTTER = $1\frac{1}{2}$ CUPS

10.25-OUNCE JAR LOW SUGAR = 1 CUP

15.5-OUNCE JAR LOW SUGAR = $1\frac{1}{2}$ CUPS

10-OUNCE JAR SIMPLY FRUIT = 1 SCANT CUP

14.25-OUNCE JAR SIMPLY FRUIT = $1\frac{1}{3}$ CUPS

5-OUNCE JAR NUTS IN SYRUP = $\frac{1}{2}$ CUP

12-OUNCE JAR TOPPING = 1 CUP

18-OUNCE JAR TOPPING = $1\frac{1}{2}$ CUPS

16-OUNCE BOTTLE TOPPING = $1\frac{1}{3}$ CUPS

20-OUNCE BOTTLE TOPPING = $1\frac{3}{4}$ CUPS

12-OUNCE BOTTLE FRUIT SYRUPS = $1\frac{1}{2}$ CUPS

12-OUNCE JAR NATURAL PEANUT BUTTER = $1\frac{1}{4}$ CUPS

16-OUNCE JAR NATURAL PEANUT BUTTER = $1\frac{3}{4}$ CUPS

SHRIMP AND SNOW PEA APPETIZERS WITH CURRANT MUSTARD SAUCE PAGE 8

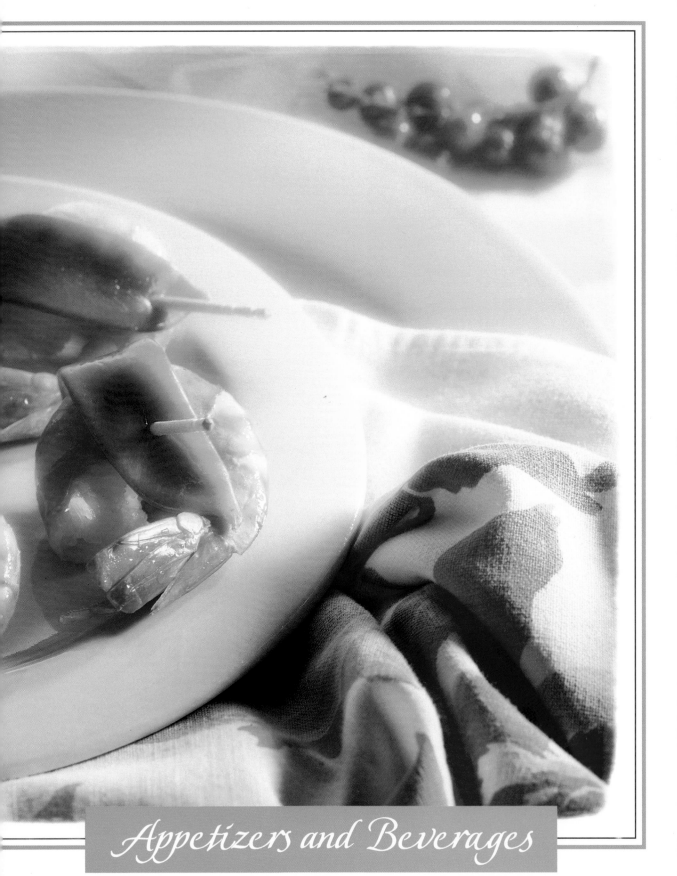

Appetizers and Beverages

SHRIMP AND SNOW PEA APPETIZERS
WITH CURRANT MUSTARD SAUCE

Shrimp and Snow Pea Appetizers with Currant Mustard Sauce

36 appetizers

6 OUNCES FRESH SNOW PEAS
   (ABOUT 36)
1 1/2 POUNDS MEDIUM SHRIMP,
   COOKED AND PEELED

CURRANT MUSTARD SAUCE
   3/4 CUP **SMUCKER'S** CURRANT JELLY
   1/4 CUP DIJON MUSTARD

Blanch snow peas in boiling salted water for 45 seconds from second boil. Immediately drain and run under cold water.

Wrap 1 blanched pea pod around each shrimp and secure with toothpick.

Combine jelly and mustard; beat with a fork or wire whisk. (Jelly will dissolve in 5 minutes or so and sauce will be smooth.) Serve sauce with appetizers.

CONTEST WINNER

Sweet and Sour Meatballs

4 to 6 servings

MEATBALLS
- ½ CUP INSTANT RICE
- 2 POUNDS LEAN GROUND BEEF
- 1 EGG
- 1 CUP SOFT BUTTER-FLAVORED CRACKER CRUMBS*
- 2 TABLESPOONS OIL

SAUCE
- 1½ CUPS BARBECUE SAUCE
- 1 CUP (12-OUNCE JAR) **SMUCKER'S** PINEAPPLE TOPPING
- ¼ CUP FIRMLY PACKED BROWN SUGAR

Prepare rice according to package directions.

Meanwhile, combine ground beef, egg and cracker crumbs; mix well. Add cooked rice; mix thoroughly. Shape into 1½ or 2-inch meatballs. Cook in oil over medium heat until browned, turning occasionally. If necessary, drain grease from skillet.

Combine all sauce ingredients; mix until brown sugar is dissolved. Pour over meatballs. Cover and simmer over low heat for 30 to 45 minutes or until meatballs are no longer pink in center. Serve with toothpicks.

Note: *You may substitute croutons or stuffing mix for the crackers.

Jenese "Nikki" Fraley
Laboratory Technician
The J.M. Smucker Company
Orrville, Ohio
Employee since 1985

"Even the best recipe needs a personal touch – in this case, pineapple topping. The result is delicious, just ask my picky eaters!"

Raspberry Mushroom Kabobs

12 kabobs

- 1 POUND BUTTON MUSHROOMS
- 1 CUP (12-OUNCE JAR) **SMUCKER'S** RED RASPBERRY PRESERVES
- ½ CUP RED WINE VINEGAR
- 1 TEASPOON MUSTARD
- 1 CLOVE GARLIC, MINCED
- 1 TABLESPOON CHOPPED PARSLEY SALT AND PEPPER, TO TASTE

Remove mushroom stems and reserve for another use. Blanch mushroom caps in boiling salted water for 5 minutes.

Dissolve preserves in red wine vinegar. Stir in mustard, garlic, parsley, salt and pepper. Drain cooked mushrooms and add to sauce to cool. (Recipe can be prepared to this point up to 3 days in advance.)

Thread 3 to 4 mushrooms on each of 12 skewers. Place skewers on preheated grill. Cook for 3 minutes on each side before serving.

Cheese Tortellini Twirls with Peach Sauce

16 kabobs

2 (9-OUNCE) PACKAGES
   FRESH CHEESE TORTELLINI
1 CUP (12-OUNCE JAR) **SMUCKER'S**
   PEACH PRESERVES
¼ CUP RED WINE VINEGAR
1 TEASPOON CHOPPED GARLIC
¼ TEASPOON PEPPER
2 TABLESPOONS TOMATO PASTE
½ CUP DICED BLACK OLIVES
¼ CUP CHOPPED PARSLEY OR BASIL

Cook tortellini as directed on package.

Thread 3 tortellini on each of 16 skewers. Place in shallow tray.

Combine all remaining ingredients except parsley; pour over tortellini. Marinate overnight in refrigerator.

Serve cold or heat at 350° for 12 to 15 minutes. Serve garnished with parsley.

CHEESE TORTELLINI TWIRLS WITH PEACH SAUCE

PICTURED LEFT TO RIGHT: RED RASPBERRY MULLED CIDER PAGE 15, HEAT WAVE PUNCH PAGE 14,
CITRUS PINEAPPLE PUNCH PAGE 13

Citrus Pineapple Punch

24 (¹/₂-cup) servings

- 1 (12-OUNCE) CAN FROZEN PINEAPPLE JUICE CONCENTRATE, THAWED
- 3 CUPS WATER
- ¼ CUP LEMON JUICE
- ½ CUP **SMUCKER'S** SWEET ORANGE MARMALADE
- 1 (32-OUNCE) BOTTLE ORANGE-FLAVORED SELTZER WATER
- 1 PINT ORANGE SHERBET
- ½ CUP MARASCHINO CHERRIES ORANGE SLICES, IF DESIRED

In punch bowl or pitcher, combine pineapple juice concentrate, water, lemon juice and marmalade; stir to combine. Add seltzer, blending well. Stir in sherbet and maraschino cherries. Chill at least 1 hour. Serve over ice; garnish drinks with orange slices.

Mulled Apricot Punch

11 (¹/₂-cup) servings

- 4 CUPS WATER
- 3 TO 5 WHOLE CLOVES
- 1 CINNAMON STICK
- 1½ CUPS (12-OUNCE BOTTLE) **SMUCKER'S** NATURAL APRICOT SYRUP
- ¼ CUP LEMON JUICE
- 1 LEMON, THINLY SLICED

Bring water, cloves and cinnamon stick to a boil. Cover; simmer for 30 minutes.

Just before serving, stir in syrup and lemon juice. Place slice of lemon in each cup. Pour hot punch through strainer into cups. Serve immediately.

RED RASPBERRY MULLED CIDER, HEAT WAVE PUNCH

Heat Wave Punch

20 (½-cup) servings

JUICE OF 2 LEMONS

JUICE OF 2 LIMES

2 TABLESPOONS CHOPPED FRESH
GINGER OR ½ TEASPOON
GROUND GINGER

1 CUP (12-OUNCE JAR) **SMUCKER'S**
STRAWBERRY JELLY

4 CUPS CRANBERRY JUICE

4 CUPS SELTZER WATER

LEMON OR LIME SLICES,
IF DESIRED

Combine lemon and lime juices, ginger and
jelly in small saucepan or microwaveable bowl.
Heat mixture over medium heat and simmer
for 5 minutes, stirring twice to help jelly
dissolve. Or heat mixture in microwave
oven on High for 2 minutes until jelly
dissolves. Cool.

Combine cooled mixture, cranberry juice and
seltzer. Pour over crushed ice; garnish drinks
with lemon and lime slices.

Red Raspberry Mulled Cider

12 (½-cup) servings

- 4 CUPS APPLE CIDER OR APPLE JUICE
- ½ CUP **SMUCKER'S** SEEDLESS RED RASPBERRY JAM
- 2 TEASPOONS LEMON JUICE
  CINNAMON STICKS, RED OR GREEN APPLE SLICES, AND/OR WHOLE CRANBERRIES, IF DESIRED

In medium non-aluminum saucepan, combine cider and jam. With a wire whisk, stir to dissolve the jam. Simmer over medium-low heat for 5 minutes, or until warm.

Stir in lemon juice; pour into heated mugs. Garnish with cinnamon sticks, apple slices and/or cranberries.

Note: Mulled cider may be prepared in advance and reheated in a microwave oven in individual cups. Or keep it warm in an electric crock pot.

Berry Punch

32 (½-cup) servings

- 1½ CUPS (12-OUNCE BOTTLE) **SMUCKER'S** NATURAL BOYSENBERRY SYRUP
- 1½ CUPS (12-OUNCE BOTTLE) **SMUCKER'S** NATURAL RED RASPBERRY SYRUP
- 4 CUPS CRANBERRY JUICE COCKTAIL
- 8 CUPS GRAPEFRUIT SODA, CHILLED
  ICE RING OR CUBES

Combine boysenberry syrup, raspberry syrup and cranberry juice. Chill until ready to serve.

To serve, pour chilled berry mixture into punch bowl. Slowly add soda. Stir gently to blend. Add ice ring or cubes. Serve immediately.

Hot Raspberry Mocha Punch

1 (1¼-cup) serving

- 2 TABLESPOONS **SMUCKER'S** SEEDLESS RED RASPBERRY JAM
- 2 TABLESPOONS **SMUCKER'S** CHOCOLATE **SUNDAE SYRUP**
- ½ CUP MILK
- ½ CUP STRONG COFFEE

In large mug, combine jam and syrup. Stir in milk and coffee.

Microwave on High for 1½ to 2 minutes; stir. Microwave 30 seconds longer or until steaming.

Glazed Meatballs

About 5 dozen meatballs

1 POUND GROUND BEEF
1/2 CUP FINE DRY BREADCRUMBS
1/3 CUP MINCED ONION
1/4 CUP MILK
1 EGG, BEATEN
1 TABLESPOON CHOPPED PARSLEY
1 TEASPOON SALT
1/2 TEASPOON WORCESTERSHIRE SAUCE
1/8 TEASPOON PEPPER
2 TABLESPOONS OIL
1/2 CUP BOTTLED CHILI SAUCE
1 CUP (12-OUNCE JAR) **SMUCKER'S** GRAPE JELLY

Combine ground beef, breadcrumbs, onion, milk, egg, parsley, salt, Worcestershire sauce and pepper; mix well. Shape into 1-inch meatballs. Cook in hot oil over medium heat for 10 to 15 minutes or until browned. Drain on paper towels.

Combine chili sauce and jelly in medium saucepan; stir well. Add meatballs; simmer 30 minutes, stirring occasionally. Serve in a chafing dish.

Spicy Apricot Chicken Wings

8 to 10 servings

2 POUNDS CHICKEN WINGS
1 CUP (12-OUNCE JAR) **SMUCKER'S** APRICOT PRESERVES
2 TABLESPOONS CIDER VINEGAR
1 TO 2 TEASPOONS HOT PEPPER SAUCE
1 TEASPOON CHILI POWDER
1 CLOVE GARLIC, MINCED

Cut off and discard chicken wing tips. Cut each wing in half at joint. Place in plastic bag; set aside.

Combine preserves, vinegar, hot pepper sauce (2 teaspoons for extra hot sauce), chili powder and garlic. Pour 1/2 cup of sauce in plastic bag with chicken; seal bag and marinate at least 1 hour or overnight. Refrigerate remaining sauce, to use for dipping when served.

Place chicken wings on preheated grill. (Reserve marinade.) Cook for 25 to 30 minutes, brushing chicken with reserved marinade during the last 5 minutes of cooking.

Discard marinade. Serve with remaining refrigerated sauce.

Note: The marinade/sauce also works well with one pound of cooked bite-size meatballs or cooked large shrimp. Marinate the cooked meatballs or shrimp as directed above. Grill them only until heated through, about 5 minutes.

GLAZED MEATBALLS, SPICY APRICOT CHICKEN WINGS

PICTURED CLOCKWISE FROM TOP: BREAKFAST BLOSSOMS PAGE 20, ORANGE MARMALADE BREAD PAGE 27, ORANGE-CREAM CHEESE MUFFINS PAGE 26

Breads

BREAKFAST BLOSSOMS

Breakfast Blossoms

10 rolls

1 (12-OUNCE) CAN BUTTERMILK
   BISCUITS (10 ROLLS)
¾ CUP **SMUCKER'S** STRAWBERRY
   PRESERVES
¼ TEASPOON CINNAMON
¼ TEASPOON NUTMEG

Grease ten 2½ or 3-inch muffin cups. Separate dough into 10 biscuits. Separate each biscuit into 3 even sections or leaves. Stand 3 sections evenly around sides and bottom of cup, overlapping slightly. Press dough edges firmly together.

Combine preserves, cinnamon and nutmeg; place scant tablespoonful in center of each cup.

Bake at 375° for 10 to 12 minutes or until lightly browned. Cool slightly before removing from pan. Serve warm.

Raspberry Crumb Coffee Cake

12 to 16 servings

COFFEE CAKE

- 1 (18.25-OUNCE) PACKAGE DELUXE WHITE CAKE MIX
- 1 CUP ALL-PURPOSE FLOUR
- 1 PACKAGE (1/4-OUNCE) ACTIVE DRY YEAST
- 2/3 CUP WARM WATER
- 2 EGGS
- 1 1/2 CUPS (18-OUNCE JAR) **SMUCKER'S** RED RASPBERRY PRESERVES
- 1/4 CUP SUGAR
- 1 TEASPOON CINNAMON
- 6 TABLESPOONS BUTTER OR MARGARINE

TOPPING

- 1 CUP POWDERED SUGAR
- 1 TABLESPOON CORN SYRUP
- 1 TO 3 TABLESPOONS MILK

Grease 13x9-inch pan. Reserve 2 1/2 cups dry cake mix. Combine remaining cake mix, flour, yeast, water and eggs. Mix by hand 100 strokes. Spread batter in greased pan. Spoon preserves evenly over batter.

Combine reserved cake mix, sugar and cinnamon; cut in butter with fork until fine particles form. Sprinkle over preserves.

Bake at 375° for 30 to 35 minutes or until golden brown.

Combine all topping ingredients, adding enough milk for desired drizzling consistency. Drizzle over warm or cooled coffee cake.

Apricot-Peanut Butter Muffins

10 muffins

- 1 3/4 CUPS ALL-PURPOSE FLOUR
- 2 1/2 TEASPOONS BAKING POWDER
- 2 1/2 TABLESPOONS SUGAR
- 3/4 TEASPOON SALT
- 1/4 CUP SHORTENING
- 1/4 CUP **SMUCKER'S** CREAMY NATURAL PEANUT BUTTER OR **LAURA SCUDDER'S** SMOOTH OLD-FASHIONED PEANUT BUTTER
- 1 EGG, WELL BEATEN
- 3/4 CUP MILK
- 2 TABLESPOONS **SMUCKER'S** APRICOT PRESERVES

Grease 10 large muffin cups. Combine flour, baking powder, sugar and salt; cut in shortening and peanut butter. Mix egg and milk together and add all at once to dry ingredients. Stir only until dry ingredients are moistened. Fill muffin cups 2/3 full. Spoon about 1/2 teaspoon preserves in center of each muffin.

Bake at 400° for 25 minutes or until done.

Breakfast Popover

4 servings

POPOVER
- ½ CUP ALL-PURPOSE FLOUR
- ½ CUP SKIM MILK
- 4 EGG WHITES
- 1 TABLESPOON BUTTER OR MARGARINE, MELTED
- ⅛ TEASPOON SALT

TOPPING
- 1½ CUPS CHOPPED APPLES
- ½ CUP **SMUCKER'S** APPLE JELLY
- 2 TABLESPOONS WATER
- ⅛ TEASPOON CINNAMON

Coat 8-inch square pan with nonstick cooking spray. In medium bowl whisk together flour and milk. Whisk in egg whites, butter and salt. Pour into pan.

Bake at 400° for 25 to 30 minutes or until puffed and golden brown.

Meanwhile, combine all topping ingredients in small saucepan; cook over low heat until apples are tender and mixture is hot, stirring frequently. Immediately after removing popover from oven, cut into fourths and serve with hot topping.

BREAKFAST POPOVER

Stuffed French Toast

10 to 12 slices

1 (8-OUNCE) PACKAGE CREAM CHEESE, SOFTENED
2 TABLESPOONS SUGAR
1½ TEASPOONS VANILLA
¼ TEASPOON CINNAMON
½ CUP CHOPPED WALNUTS OR PECANS
1 (1-POUND) LOAF FRENCH BREAD
4 EGGS
1 CUP WHIPPING CREAM OR HALF AND HALF
½ TEASPOON NUTMEG
1 CUP (12-OUNCE JAR) **SMUCKER'S** APRICOT PRESERVES
½ CUP ORANGE JUICE
½ TEASPOON ALMOND EXTRACT FRESH FRUIT

Beat together cream cheese, sugar, 1 teaspoon of the vanilla and cinnamon until fluffy. Stir in nuts; set aside.

Cut bread into 10 to 12 (1½-inch) slices; cut pocket in top of each. Fill each pocket with about 1½ tablespoons of cream cheese mixture.

Beat together eggs, whipping cream, remaining ½ teaspoon vanilla and nutmeg. Using tongs, dip bread slices in egg mixture, being careful not to squeeze out filling. Cook on a lightly greased griddle until both sides are golden brown. (To keep cooked slices hot for serving, place on baking sheet in warm oven.)

Meanwhile, combine and heat preserves and orange juice. Stir in almond extract. To serve, drizzle apricot mixture over French toast. Serve with fresh fruit.

STUFFED FRENCH TOAST

ORANGE-CREAM CHEESE MUFFINS,
ORANGE MARMALADE BREAD

Orange-Cream Cheese Muffins

12 muffins

MUFFINS

1 3/4	CUPS ALL-PURPOSE FLOUR
2 1/2	TEASPOONS BAKING POWDER
1/4	CUP SUGAR
1/2	TEASPOON SALT
1/4	CUP CHOPPED NUTS
1	EGG
1/3	CUP ORANGE JUICE
1/3	CUP **SMUCKER'S** SWEET ORANGE MARMALADE
1/4	CUP MILK
1/4	CUP OIL

FROSTING

1 1/2	OUNCES CREAM CHEESE, SOFTENED
2	CUPS POWDERED SUGAR
1/4	CUP **SMUCKER'S** SWEET ORANGE MARMALADE
1 TO 2	TEASPOONS MILK

Grease bottom only of 12 muffin cups. Combine flour, baking powder, sugar and salt into bowl. Add nuts; mix well. Make well in center. Combine egg, orange juice, marmalade, milk and oil. Add all at once to dry ingredients. Stir quickly just until dry ingredients are moistened.

Fill greased muffin cups 2/3 full. Bake at 425° for 20 to 25 minutes. Cool.

Combine all frosting ingredients; mix well. Frost cooled muffins.

Orange Marmalade Bread

8 to 10 servings

3 CUPS ALL-PURPOSE FLOUR,
   STIRRED BEFORE MEASURING
4 TEASPOONS BAKING POWDER
1 TEASPOON SALT
1/2 CUP CHOPPED WALNUTS
2 EGGS, LIGHTLY BEATEN
2 TABLESPOONS OIL
1/4 CUP HONEY
3/4 CUP **SMUCKER'S** SWEET
   ORANGE MARMALADE
3/4 CUP MILK

Grease 9x5x3-inch loaf pan. Combine flour, baking powder and salt into large bowl. Stir in nuts. Combine eggs, oil, honey, marmalade and milk; blend well. Add to flour mixture; stir only until dry ingredients are moistened (batter will be lumpy). Turn into prepared pan.

Bake at 350° for 65 to 70 minutes or until lightly browned and toothpick inserted in center comes out clean.

Blueberry Coffee Cake

9 servings

COFFEE CAKE
1 1/2 CUPS ALL-PURPOSE FLOUR
1/4 CUP SUGAR
2 1/2 TEASPOONS BAKING POWDER
1/2 TEASPOON SALT
1/4 TEASPOON GROUND ALLSPICE
1/3 CUP BUTTER OR MARGARINE,
   MELTED
1 EGG
2/3 CUP MILK
3/4 CUP **SMUCKER'S** BLUEBERRY
   PRESERVES

TOPPING
1/4 CUP FIRMLY PACKED
   BROWN SUGAR
1/4 CUP CHOPPED WALNUTS
2 TABLESPOONS FLOUR
1 TABLESPOON BUTTER OR
   MARGARINE

Grease and flour 8 or 9-inch square baking pan. Lightly spoon flour into measuring cup; level off. In medium bowl, combine 1 1/2 cups flour, sugar, baking powder, salt and allspice. Add melted butter, egg and milk. Mix vigorously until well blended.

Pour half of batter into greased and floured pan; spread preserves evenly over batter. Top with remaining batter.

Combine topping ingredients; mix until crumbly. Sprinkle over top of coffee cake.

Bake at 400° for 20 to 25 minutes or until toothpick inserted in center comes out clean.

Raspberry Breakfast Braid

10 to 12 servings

COFFEE CAKE

- 2 CUPS PACKAGED BAKING MIX
- 1 (3-OUNCE) PACKAGE CREAM CHEESE
- ¼ CUP BUTTER OR MARGARINE
- ⅓ CUP MILK
- ½ CUP **SMUCKER'S** RED RASPBERRY PRESERVES

GLAZE

- 1 CUP POWDERED SUGAR
- ¼ TEASPOON ALMOND EXTRACT
- ¼ TEASPOON VANILLA
- 1 TO 2 TABLESPOONS MILK

In medium bowl, measure baking mix. Cut in cream cheese and butter until mixture is crumbly. Stir in milk. Turn dough onto a lightly floured surface and knead lightly 10 to 12 times. Roll dough into a 12 x 8-inch rectangle. Turn onto greased baking sheet. Spread preserves lengthwise down center ⅓ of dough. Make 2½-inch cuts at 1-inch intervals on long sides. Fold strips over filling.

Bake at 425° for 12 to 15 minutes or until lightly browned.

Combine all glaze ingredients, adding enough milk for desired drizzling consistency. Drizzle over coffee cake.

RASPBERRY BREAKFAST BRAID

Fruit Muffins

12 muffins

MUFFINS

2/3	CUP MILK
1	TABLESPOON OIL
1	EGG
2	CUPS PACKAGED BAKING MIX
2	TABLESPOONS SUGAR
1/4	CUP **SMUCKER'S** PRESERVES (ANY FLAVOR)

GLAZE

2/3	CUP POWDERED SUGAR
3 TO 4	TEASPOONS MILK

Grease bottom only of 12 medium muffin cups or line with paper baking cups. Combine milk, oil and egg; blend until well mixed. Add baking mix and sugar; stir just until moistened. Fill greased muffin cups 2/3 full. Drop 1 level teaspoon of preserves onto center of batter in each cup.

Bake at 400° for 13 to 18 minutes or until golden brown. Cool slightly and remove from pan.

Stir together glaze ingredients until smooth, adding enough milk for desired glaze consistency. Drizzle over cooled muffins.

Cherry Swirl Coffee Cake

2 coffee cakes

1 1/4	CUPS MILK
1/2	CUP SHORTENING OR MARGARINE
1/4	CUP SUGAR
1	TEASPOON SALT
1	PACKAGE (1/4-OUNCE) ACTIVE DRY YEAST
3 1/4	CUPS ALL-PURPOSE FLOUR
2	EGGS
1/2	TEASPOON VANILLA
1	CUP (12-OUNCE JAR) **SMUCKER'S** CHERRY PRESERVES
1	CUP POWDERED SUGAR
	MILK
1/3	CUP SLICED ALMONDS

In small saucepan, combine 1 1/4 cups milk, shortening, sugar and salt; bring just to a boil. Cool to lukewarm (105° to 115°). Stir in yeast; transfer mixture to medium bowl.

Add 1 cup of the flour to milk mixture; beat well. Add eggs and vanilla; beat well. Stir in enough of the remaining flour to make a thick batter; beat until smooth. Cover and set in warm place, free from drafts, until doubled in size, about 1 hour.

Stir batter down and pour into two greased 9-inch round cake pans; cover and set in warm place until doubled in size, about 1 hour. Make a swirl design on top of batter with a floured spoon; fill grooves with preserves, using 1/4 cup for each coffee cake.

Bake at 375° for 30 to 35 minutes or until golden brown. Remove from pans; cool slightly on wire racks. Fill grooves with remaining preserves.

Mix powdered sugar with enough milk to make a thin glaze consistency; drizzle over warm coffee cakes. Sprinkle with almonds.

Fred's Raspberry Cream Cheese Coffee Cake

12 servings

2 1/4 CUPS ALL-PURPOSE FLOUR
1 CUP SUGAR
3/4 CUP BUTTER OR MARGARINE, CUT INTO 12 PIECES
1/2 TEASPOON BAKING POWDER
1/2 TEASPOON BAKING SODA
1/4 TEASPOON SALT
3/4 CUP SOUR CREAM
2 EGGS
1 TEASPOON ALMOND EXTRACT
1 (8-OUNCE) PACKAGE CREAM CHEESE, SOFTENED
1/2 TEASPOON GRATED LEMON PEEL
1/2 TEASPOON VANILLA
1/2 CUP **SMUCKER'S** SEEDLESS RED RASPBERRY JAM
1/2 CUP SLIVERED ALMONDS

Grease and flour bottom and sides of 10-inch springform pan. In large bowl, combine flour and 3/4 cup of the sugar. Using pastry blender, cut in butter until mixture resembles coarse crumbs. Reserve 1 cup crumb mixture.

To remaining crumb mixture, add baking powder, baking soda, salt, sour cream, 1 of the eggs and almond extract; blend well. Spread batter over bottom and 2 inches up sides of prepared pan. Batter should be about 1/4-inch thick on sides.

Combine cream cheese, remaining 1/4 cup sugar, remaining egg, lemon peel and vanilla; blend well. Spread over batter in pan. Spoon jam evenly over cream cheese filling.

Combine reserved crumb mixture and almonds. Sprinkle over top.

Bake at 350° for 45 to 55 minutes or until cream cheese filling is set and crust is deep golden brown. Cool 15 minutes. Remove sides of pan. Serve warm or cool. Refrigerate leftovers.

Dave Painting
Project Leader, Management Information Systems
The J.M. Smucker Company
Orrville, Ohio
Employee since 1977

"This coffee cake looks impressive enough to have come from a bakery. For an extra fluffy texture, use a whisk to blend the cream cheese mixture."

FRUIT SALAD WITH PEANUT BUTTER DRESSING PAGE 34

Salads, Sides and Sauces

FRUIT SALAD WITH PEANUT BUTTER DRESSING

Fruit Salad with Peanut Butter Dressing

8 servings

DRESSING

1 (6-OUNCE) CAN FROZEN PINEAPPLE JUICE CONCENTRATE, THAWED
¼ CUP **SMUCKER'S** CREAMY NATURAL PEANUT BUTTER OR **LAURA SCUDDER'S** SMOOTH OLD-FASHIONED PEANUT BUTTER
½ TEASPOON LEMON JUICE
¼ TEASPOON GROUND CORIANDER
⅛ TEASPOON CAYENNE PEPPER
¾ CUP OIL

SALAD

4 CUPS TORN LETTUCE
1 CUP FRESH OR CANNED PINEAPPLE CHUNKS, DRAINED
1 (LOOSELY PACKED) CUP SLICED FRESH OR FROZEN PEACHES, THAWED* OR 1 (8-OUNCE) CAN SLICED PEACHES IN THEIR OWN JUICE, DRAINED
¼ MEDIUM CANTALOUPE, PEELED AND CUT INTO WEDGES
½ CUP HALVED SEEDLESS GREEN GRAPES
½ CUP HALVED FRESH STRAWBERRIES
½ CUP CHOPPED PEANUTS

In blender container or food processor bowl, place pineapple juice concentrate, peanut butter, lemon juice, coriander and cayenne pepper. Cover and blend until smooth. Keeping blender running at medium-high speed, gradually add oil through hole in lid or with lid ajar until mixture is well blended. Turn into storage container; cover. Store dressing in refrigerator until serving time; stir before using.

Line individual serving plates or large platter with lettuce; arrange fruit on lettuce. Drizzle with dressing; garnish with chopped peanuts.

Note: *Coat peaches with lemon juice to prevent darkening.

Smoked Turkey and Strawberry Spinach Salad

4 servings

DRESSING

- 1/2 CUP **SMUCKER'S** STRAWBERRY JELLY
- 2 TABLESPOONS RED WINE VINEGAR
- 1/2 TEASPOON GRATED LEMON PEEL

SALAD

- 4 CUPS TORN SPINACH
- 2 CUPS CUBED COOKED SMOKED TURKEY OR CHICKEN
- 1 1/3 CUPS SLICED OR HALVED FRESH STRAWBERRIES
- 1 (11-OUNCE) CAN MANDARIN ORANGES, CHILLED, DRAINED
- 2 THIN SLICES RED ONION, SEPARATED INTO RINGS

In small saucepan, combine jelly, vinegar and lemon peel. Cook over medium-high heat until jelly is melted, stirring frequently. Cool 10 minutes.

Meanwhile, arrange spinach, turkey, strawberries, oranges and onion rings on 4 individual salad plates. Serve with dressing.

Raspberry Salad

12 servings

RASPBERRY DRESSING

- 1/3 CUP **SMUCKER'S** SEEDLESS RED RASPBERRY JAM
- 1/3 CUP WHITE VINEGAR
- 1 CUP OIL

SALAD

- 4 CUPS TORN BOSTON LETTUCE
- 4 CUPS TORN RED LEAF LETTUCE
- 3/4 CUP CHOPPED WALNUTS, TOASTED
- 1 CUP FRESH RASPBERRIES
- 1 MEDIUM RED ONION, THINLY SLICED

Combine jam and vinegar in blender; process 20 seconds. With blender on high, gradually add oil in a slow, steady stream.

Combine all salad ingredients; toss gently. Serve salad with dressing.

Three Bean Salad with Sweet and Sour Apricot Dressing

6 servings

SWEET AND SOUR APRICOT DRESSING

1/2 CUP **SMUCKER'S** APRICOT PRESERVES

1/4 CUP RED WINE VINEGAR

1 TEASPOON CELERY SEED

SALAD

1 (16-OUNCE) CAN KIDNEY BEANS, DRAINED AND RINSED

1 CUP COOKED GREEN BEANS (FRESH OR FROZEN), CUT INTO 2-INCH PIECES

1 CUP COOKED YELLOW WAX BEANS (FRESH OR FROZEN), CUT INTO 2-INCH PIECES

1 SMALL RED ONION, THINLY SLICED SALT AND PEPPER

Combine preserves, vinegar and celery seed; mix well. Add kidney beans, green and yellow beans and sliced onion; toss well to combine. Season with salt and pepper. Cover and refrigerate.

THREE BEAN SALAD WITH SWEET AND SOUR APRICOT DRESSING

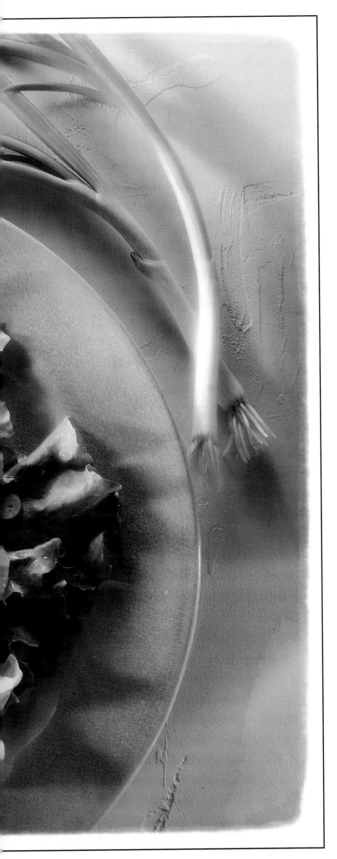

Plantation Salad

6 servings

DRESSING

- 1/2 CUP **SMUCKER'S** SWEET ORANGE MARMALADE
- JUICE OF 1 LEMON (ABOUT 1/3 CUP)
- 1/4 TEASPOON FRESHLY GROUND PEPPER
- 1/4 CUP PEANUT OR VEGETABLE OIL
- 1/3 CUP NONFAT SOUR CREAM OR PLAIN YOGURT
- 1 BUNCH GREEN ONIONS, THINLY SLICED
- 2 TABLESPOONS WHITE VINEGAR

SALAD

- 1 SMALL HEAD LEAF LETTUCE OR OTHER SALAD GREENS
- 1 LARGE RIPE AVOCADO, PEELED AND THINLY SLICED
- 1 LARGE ORANGE, PEELED AND THINLY SLICED OR SECTIONED
- 1 SMALL BERMUDA ONION, PEELED AND THINLY SLICED
- 1 SMALL FRESH PINEAPPLE, PEELED, CORED AND SLICED INTO RINGS OR BITS
- 1/4 CUP CHOPPED CASHEWS, IF DESIRED

Place marmalade and lemon juice in glass measuring cup. Microwave on High for 2 minutes or until marmalade melts. (Or heat mixture in small saucepan over medium heat.) Stir in remaining dressing ingredients. Chill before serving.

Arrange lettuce on individual serving plates or large serving platter. Top with avocado, orange, onion and pineapple. Drizzle with dressing and garnish with cashews.

PLANTATION SALAD

Cumberland Sauce

1½ cups sauce

¾ CUP **SMUCKER'S** CURRANT JELLY
1 (6-OUNCE) CAN FROZEN ORANGE
   JUICE CONCENTRATE, THAWED
1 TEASPOON DRY MUSTARD
⅛ TEASPOON GINGER
¼ TEASPOON HOT PEPPER SAUCE

Combine all ingredients in a small saucepan.
Heat the sauce until it comes to a boil, stirring
constantly. Cook 1 minute. Serve hot or cold
with chicken, duck or game.

Sweet Orange Salad Dressing

¾ cup dressing

½ CUP PLAIN NONFAT YOGURT
2 TABLESPOONS HONEY
¼ TEASPOON DRY MUSTARD
½ CUP **SMUCKER'S** SWEET ORANGE
   MARMALADE

Combine all ingredients; mix well. Refrigerate,
covered, until ready to use. Stir before using.

Note: This tangy dressing is excellent on fruit
salads and green salads.

Brown Rice Salad

6 to 8 servings

2½ CUPS WATER
1 CUP UNCOOKED BROWN RICE
¾ CUP **SMUCKER'S** GRAPE JELLY
½ CUP FRESH LEMON JUICE
¼ CUP OLIVE OIL
2 TABLESPOONS DRIED
   MINT LEAVES
½ TEASPOON SALT
1 CUP CHOPPED FRESH PARSLEY
2 CUCUMBERS, PEELED, HALVED,
   SEEDED AND DICED
1 CUP CHOPPED RED RADISHES
½ CUP CHOPPED GREEN ONIONS

In medium saucepan, bring water to a boil. Add
rice. Cover and cook over low heat for about
45 minutes or until water is absorbed and rice
is tender. Cool.

In blender container, combine jelly, lemon juice,
oil, mint and salt; cover and blend until smooth.

In straight-sided 1½-quart glass bowl or soufflé
dish, layer rice, parsley and half of cucumbers.
Pour half of dressing over layers. Add radishes,
remaining cucumbers, green onions and
remaining dressing. Refrigerate several hours or
overnight. Toss before serving.

Note: To make a bulgur salad, omit the rice
(and water). Cook 1 cup of bulgur in 2 cups of
boiling water until tender, about 15 minutes.
Continue as directed above.

Zesty Apple Butter Barbecue Sauce

3 cups sauce

- 1 CUP (11-OUNCE JAR) **SMUCKER'S** CIDER APPLE BUTTER
- 1/2 CUP KETCHUP
- 1 TABLESPOON PREPARED MUSTARD
- 1 TEASPOON WORCESTERSHIRE SAUCE
- 3 TEASPOONS LIQUID SMOKE
- 1/2 TEASPOON RED PEPPER
- 1/2 TEASPOON COARSE KOSHER SALT
- 1/2 TEASPOON FRESHLY GROUND PEPPER
- 1 CUP FINELY CHOPPED ONIONS
- 1 TEASPOON APPLE CIDER VINEGAR
- 1/2 TEASPOON MINCED GARLIC
- 1/2 CUP FIRMLY PACKED BROWN SUGAR
- 1/2 TEASPOON PAPRIKA

In large bowl, combine all ingredients. Mix well.

Add desired meat portions, making sure all pieces are well coated. Cover and marinate in refrigerator 3 to 4 hours or overnight. Bake or barbecue according to your favorite technique. Use remaining sauce to baste.

Randy Hecker
Plant Manager
The J.M. Smucker Company
Grandview, Washington
Employee since 1983

"Most barbecue sauces are tomato based. Apple butter provides a different approach with a very pleasant result."

Chicken Pasta Salad with Mint Mustard Sauce and Snow Peas

8 (1½-cup) servings

MINT MUSTARD SAUCE
- 1/2 CUP **SMUCKER'S** MINT FLAVORED APPLE JELLY
- 1/4 CUP DIJON MUSTARD
- 2 TABLESPOONS WHITE VINEGAR
- 2 TABLESPOONS CHOPPED FRESH GINGERROOT OR 1/2 TEASPOON GROUND GINGER
- 1/4 TEASPOON PEPPER

SALAD
- 1 CUP SNOW PEAS
- 3/4 TO 1 POUND BONELESS SKINLESS CHICKEN BREASTS
  PEPPER
- 1 (10-OUNCE) BOX BOW-TIE PASTA, COOKED AND COOLED
- 1 BUNCH SCALLIONS, FINELY CHOPPED (ABOUT 1/2 CUP)
- 1 HEAD OF BOSTON LETTUCE
- 1 HEAD OF RED LEAF LETTUCE

Combine all sauce ingredients in glass measuring cup; mix well. Microwave on High for 1½ minutes or until jelly melts. Cool.

Blanch snow peas in boiling salted water for 45 seconds from second boil. Immediately drain and run under cold water; halve lengthwise.

Cut chicken into 1-inch pieces. Season generously with pepper. Coat nonstick skillet with vegetable cooking spray. Heat over high heat; cook chicken about 3 minutes on each side or until lightly browned and cooked through. Remove from skillet and cool.

Combine sauce, snow peas, chicken, pasta and scallions; blend well. Season with salt and additional pepper, if desired. Serve each portion on a bed of crisp Boston and red leaf lettuce.

Corn, Vegetable and Pepper Salad with Spicy Orange Lime Dressing

12 servings

SPICY ORANGE LIME DRESSING

1/2 CUP **SMUCKER'S** SWEET ORANGE MARMALADE

1/4 CUP LIME JUICE, AND THE JUICE OF 1 LIME

1/4 TEASPOON BLACK PEPPER

1/4 TEASPOON CAYENNE PEPPER

SALAD

1 CUP COOKED CORN

1 LARGE WHITE ONION, DICED

1 TOMATO, FINELY CHOPPED

1 GREEN BELL PEPPER, FINELY CHOPPED

3 CUPS COOKED RICE

2 (12-OUNCE) CANS WHOLE MILD CHILE PEPPERS

1 LARGE BAG TORTILLA CHIPS, IF DESIRED

Combine all dressing ingredients; mix well. Combine corn, onion, tomato, green pepper and cooked rice. Add dressing; toss to coat.

Slice whole peppers horizontally and fill each half with rice mixture; place on decorative platter. Serve with remaining rice mixture and tortilla chips.

CORN, VEGETABLE AND PEPPER SALAD WITH SPICY ORANGE LIME DRESSING

Waldorf Salad with Turkey and Apricot

6 servings

DRESSING

1/3 CUP **SMUCKER'S** APRICOT
    PRESERVES

1/2 CUP NONFAT PLAIN YOGURT

1 TABLESPOON CHOPPED
    DRIED TARRAGON, CHIVES,
    PARSLEY OR CURRY POWDER

1 TEASPOON DIJON MUSTARD

2 TABLESPOONS LEMON JUICE

1/2 TEASPOON GRATED LEMON PEEL

1/2 TEASPOON SALT

1/8 TEASPOON FRESHLY
    GROUND PEPPER

SALAD

1 POUND BONELESS SKINLESS
    TURKEY OR CHICKEN,
    COOKED AND CUBED*

1 CUP DICED UNPEELED RED APPLE
    (1/2-INCH PIECES)

1 CUP DICED UNPEELED GREEN
    APPLE (1/2-INCH PIECES)

1 CUP DICED CELERY
    (1/4-INCH PIECES)

1/4 CUP RAISINS

6 LETTUCE LEAVES

1 TABLESPOON CHOPPED FRESH
    PARSLEY OR CHIVES

Combine all dressing ingredients; stir until well blended. Add turkey or chicken, apples, celery and raisins. Toss to coat the salad ingredients.

Season with additional salt and/or pepper, if desired.

Place lettuce leaf on each of 6 serving plates. Top each with mound of salad. Garnish each salad with chopped fresh parsley or chives.

Notes: *Deli turkey breast may be used in this recipe. Ask the deli to slice the turkey into 3/4 or 1-inch slices, then cube the meat at home before adding it to this salad.

This also makes an excellent sandwich filling for pita (pocket) breads.

Apricot-Pineapple Mold

8 to 10 servings

- ½ CUP **SMUCKER'S** APRICOT PRESERVES
- ½ CUP **SMUCKER'S** PINEAPPLE TOPPING
- 2 TABLESPOONS VINEGAR
- 2½ CUPS WATER
- 1 TEASPOON WHOLE CLOVES
- 1 (4-INCH) STICK CINNAMON
- 2 (3-OUNCE) PACKAGES ORANGE-FLAVOR GELATIN
- ½ CUP SOUR CREAM

In saucepan, combine preserves, pineapple topping, vinegar and water. Tie cloves and cinnamon in small square of cheesecloth and place in saucepan. Simmer mixture over low heat for 10 minutes. Remove spice bag.

Dissolve 1 package of gelatin in 2 cups of preserve mixture; stir until dissolved. Pour into a 6-cup mold and refrigerate until almost firm.

Meanwhile, dissolve remaining package of gelatin in remaining preserve mixture; stir until dissolved. Refrigerate until partially set. Beat with an electric mixer until fluffy. Fold in sour cream. Pour over first layer in ring mold. Refrigerate until firm, about 8 hours or overnight. Unmold to serve.

Pineapple Yam Casserole

4 servings

- 4 MEDIUM YAMS, COOKED, PEELED AND MASHED, OR 2 (16 OR 17-OUNCE) CANS YAMS, DRAINED AND MASHED
- ⅓ CUP **SMUCKER'S** PINEAPPLE TOPPING
- 4 TABLESPOONS BUTTER OR MARGARINE, MELTED
- 1 TABLESPOON LEMON JUICE

Combine yams, pineapple topping, 3 tablespoons of the butter and lemon juice; mix well. Brush 1-quart casserole with remaining tablespoon butter. Spoon yam mixture into casserole.

Bake at 350° for 25 minutes or until heated through.

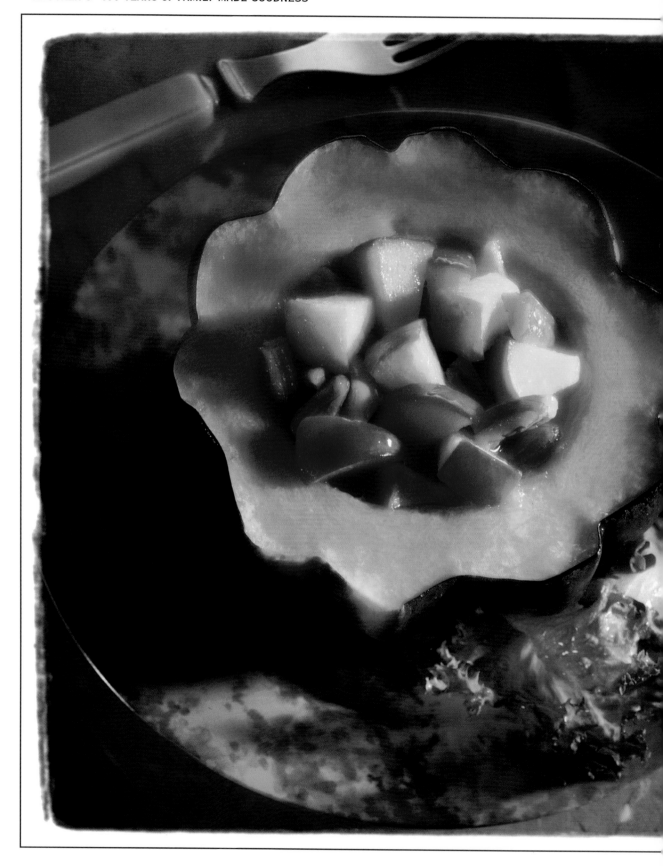

Baked Squash

4 servings

- 2 MEDIUM-SIZED ACORN SQUASH
- 2 TART RED APPLES, DICED
- 1/2 CUP CHOPPED NUTS
- 1/2 CUP **SMUCKER'S** APPLE JELLY
- 1/4 CUP BUTTER OR MARGARINE, SOFTENED

Cut squash in half crosswise or lengthwise; scoop out centers. Place in baking pan. Combine apples, nuts, jelly and butter. Fill squash with mixture. Pour a small amount of boiling water in bottom of pan around squash. Cover pan with foil.

Bake at 400° for 45 to 60 minutes or until fork-tender. Remove foil during last 5 minutes of baking.

Oriental Orange Salad

4 servings

ORIENTAL ORANGE DRESSING

- ¾ CUP **SMUCKER'S** SWEET ORANGE MARMALADE
- 2 TABLESPOONS SESAME OIL
- 2 TABLESPOONS RICE VINEGAR
- 1 TABLESPOON WATER
- ¼ TEASPOON SALT
- ⅛ TEASPOON GINGER
  DASH CAYENNE OR WHITE PEPPER

SALAD

- 2 CUPS CHOPPED (LARGE PIECES OR CUBES) COOKED CHICKEN
- 2 RED BELL PEPPERS, SEEDED AND SLICED INTO RINGS
- 4 STALKS CELERY, DIAGONALLY SLICED
- ½ POUND SNOW PEAS, BLANCHED
- 4 OUNCES BEAN OR ALFALFA SPROUTS
- 1 (8-OUNCE) CAN SLICED WATER CHESTNUTS, DRAINED

Combine all dressing ingredients in blender; cover and blend until smooth. Pour into small bowl; chill.

Chill all salad ingredients. Arrange on 4 individual serving plates or on large platter. Serve with dressing.

Note: The dressing can also be heated and served hot as a sauce for cooked poultry, meat or seafood.

Apple Buttered Sweet Potatoes

6 servings

- 1 POUND SWEET POTATOES, COOKED, PEELED AND SLICED
- 1 CUP (11-OUNCE JAR) **SMUCKER'S** CIDER APPLE BUTTER
- ⅓ CUP **SMUCKER'S** PINEAPPLE TOPPING
- 2 TABLESPOONS BUTTER OR MARGARINE, MELTED
- ½ TEASPOON SALT
- ¼ TEASPOON CINNAMON
- ¼ TEASPOON PAPRIKA

Arrange sliced sweet potatoes in ungreased shallow baking dish. Combine apple butter and remaining ingredients; mix well. Drizzle mixture over sweet potatoes.

Bake at 350° for 20 to 30 minutes or until heated through.

APPLE BUTTERED SWEET POTATOES

Green Beans Orange

6 servings

1 POUND FRESH OR
2 (9-OUNCE) PACKAGES FROZEN
WHOLE GREEN BEANS
1/4 CUP **SMUCKER'S** LOW SUGAR
ORANGE MARMALADE
1 TEASPOON LEMON JUICE

Cut ends off green beans; wash. Cover and cook in a small amount of boiling salted water until tender-crisp, about 5 minutes. Drain. (Or cook frozen green beans according to package directions; drain.)

Add marmalade and lemon juice. Cook and gently stir until beans are coated and hot.

Note: For extra interest, try:
Green Beans Anise: Add 1/4 teaspoon anise seed to marmalade.
Green Beans Piquant: Add 1/2 teaspoon celery seed to marmalade.

Tangy Orange Red Pepper Relish

1 1/2 cups relish

4 LARGE RED BELL PEPPERS,
ROASTED, SKINNED AND
COARSELY CHOPPED OR
1 (15-OUNCE) JAR ROASTED
RED PEPPERS, DRAINED
2 TABLESPOONS CIDER VINEGAR
1 CLOVE GARLIC
1/2 CUP **SMUCKER'S** SWEET
ORANGE MARMALADE
1 TABLESPOON CORNSTARCH
2 TABLESPOONS COLD WATER
1 TEASPOON HOT PEPPER SAUCE

In food processor or blender, place red peppers, vinegar and garlic; purée into smooth paste. Add marmalade; blend. Pour relish into small saucepan.

Dissolve cornstarch in cold water; stir into relish. Simmer over high heat for 5 minutes or until slightly thickened. Remove from heat; stir in hot pepper sauce. Pour relish into serving bowl; cool.

Notes: To skin red peppers, cut in half and remove seeds. Place cut-side-down on broiler pan. Broil for 10 minutes or until skin is charred. When cool, peel skin from peppers.

Serve this relish with grilled hot dogs or with your favorite grilled meats, poultry or fish.

Apricot Carrots

4 servings

1 POUND PEELED MINI CARROTS
2 TABLESPOONS WATER
1 TABLESPOON BUTTER
  OR MARGARINE, MELTED
1/2 CUP **SMUCKER'S** APRICOT
  PRESERVES
1 TABLESPOON LEMON JUICE
1/2 TEASPOON SALT
1/8 TEASPOON MACE

Cook carrots, covered, in small amount of boiling salted water for about 8 minutes or until tender. Drain thoroughly; return to pan.

Combine butter, preserves, lemon juice, salt and mace. Pour over cooked carrots. Cook, stirring constantly until carrots are evenly glazed and heated through.

APRICOT CARROTS, RASPBERRY-GLAZED TURKEY PAGE 64

Orange Chili Barbecue Sauce

2 cups sauce

1 CUP (12-OUNCE JAR) **SMUCKER'S** SWEET ORANGE MARMALADE

1 CUP TOMATO SAUCE OR CRUSHED TOMATOES PACKED IN TOMATO PURÉE

2 TABLESPOONS RED WINE VINEGAR

2 TABLESPOONS CHILI POWDER

1 TEASPOON GROUND CUMIN

1 TEASPOON FRESH CHOPPED GARLIC

1/2 TEASPOON SALT

1/4 TEASPOON CAYENNE PEPPER OR HOT PEPPER SAUCE (FOR SPICIER SAUCE)

Combine all ingredients in small saucepan; mix well. Heat until sauce comes to a boil, stirring constantly. Simmer for 1 minute. Use immediately, or cool and store in refrigerator.

Notes: To make barbecue sauce in microwave, combine all ingredients in microwave-safe bowl; mix well. Cover with plastic wrap and microwave on High for 2 minutes. Stir. Cover and microwave on High for 1 minute more.

Use the sauce as a marinade or baste for baked or grilled chicken, ribs, beef or pork.

BROILED SEA SCALLOPS WITH APRICOT CHUTNEY PAGE 56

Main Dishes

APRICOT CHUTNEY

Broiled Sea Scallops with Apricot Chutney

4 servings

APRICOT CHUTNEY

1/2 CUP **SMUCKER'S** APRICOT PRESERVES

1/4 CUP HORSERADISH

1/2 TEASPOON COARSE GROUND PEPPER

SCALLOPS

12 SLICES BACON

12 LARGE SEA SCALLOPS (1 TO 1 1/2 OUNCES EACH)

4 BAMBOO SKEWERS

2 TABLESPOONS BUTTER, MELTED SPINACH LEAVES, WASHED AND STEMS REMOVED

2 LEMONS, HALVED LEMON WEDGES, FOR GARNISH

Combine all chutney ingredients; mix well. Set aside.

Place bacon slices on wire rack in baking dish. Bake at 350° until half done, approximately 13 minutes. Wrap bacon slice around edge of each scallop; thread 3 scallops on each skewer, leaving a 1-inch gap between scallops.

Place skewers in buttered metal pie pan; brush scallops lightly with melted butter. Broil for 8 minutes or until scallops turn opaque, turning once. Meanwhile, scoop out lemon pulp from each lemon half.

To serve, place two spinach leaves and one lemon half on each of 4 serving plates. Spoon apricot chutney into each lemon half. Remove scallops from skewers and place 3 scallops on one spinach leaf on each of the plates. Garnish with lemon wedges. Serve immediately.

Note: The apricot chutney will keep in the refrigerator for up to three weeks.

Apricot Lemon Sole

4 servings

FISH FILLETS

1 EGG
1 TABLESPOON WATER
1/2 CUP CORN FLAKE CRUMBS
1/4 TEASPOON SALT
1/4 TEASPOON PAPRIKA
1/8 TEASPOON PEPPER
4 SMALL FILLETS OF SOLE
  OR FLOUNDER

APRICOT LEMON SAUCE

2/3 CUP **SMUCKER'S** LOW SUGAR
  APRICOT PRESERVES
1 TABLESPOON LEMON JUICE
1 TEASPOON PREPARED MUSTARD
1/2 TEASPOON GRATED LEMON PEEL
1/8 TEASPOON SALT

Coat baking sheet with nonstick cooking spray. In pie plate, combine egg and water. In plastic bag, combine crumbs, salt, paprika and pepper. Dip each fish fillet into egg mixture; drop into bag and shake to coat with crumbs. Arrange fish in single layer on baking sheet.

Bake at 425° for 10 minutes or until fish flakes easily with a fork. (Do not turn fish.)

Meanwhile, in small saucepan combine all sauce ingredients; heat until bubbly. Serve sauce with fish.

Pork and Peach Bake

4 servings

1 (6-OUNCE) PACKAGE
  STUFFING MIX
1/2 CUP **SMUCKER'S** PEACH
  PRESERVES
4 PORK CHOPS (1/2-INCH THICK)
2 TABLESPOONS OIL
1 (8-OUNCE) CAN SLICED
  PEACHES, DRAINED
PARSLEY

Make stuffing mix according to package directions, decreasing water by 1/4 cup; stir in 1/4 cup of the preserves. Spoon stuffing into ungreased 1-quart casserole.

Brown pork chops in oil over medium heat. Arrange pork chops and peaches over stuffing. Spoon remaining 1/4 cup preserves over chops.

Cover and bake at 350° for 45 minutes to 1 hour or until pork chops are tender. Garnish with parsley.

Mandarin Shrimp and Vegetable Stir-Fry

4 to 6 servings

1 CUP (12-OUNCE JAR) **SMUCKER'S** SWEET ORANGE MARMALADE

3 TABLESPOONS SOY SAUCE

2 TABLESPOONS WHITE VINEGAR

2 TEASPOONS HOT PEPPER SAUCE

1 1/2 TABLESPOONS CORNSTARCH

2 TABLESPOONS OIL

1 TABLESPOON CHOPPED FRESH GINGERROOT

1 TABLESPOON CHOPPED FRESH GARLIC

24 FRESH LARGE SHRIMP, PEELED AND DEVEINED

1 RED BELL PEPPER, CHOPPED

1 YELLOW OR GREEN BELL PEPPER, CHOPPED

3 CUPS BROCCOLI FLORETS

1/2 CUP WATER

1 CUP CHOPPED GREEN ONIONS

HOT COOKED RICE, IF DESIRED

Combine marmalade, soy sauce, vinegar, hot pepper sauce and cornstarch; stir to dissolve cornstarch. Set aside.

Place large skillet or wok over high heat for 1 minute, then add oil. Heat oil for 30 seconds, then add gingerroot, garlic and shrimp. Stir-fry for 2 to 3 minutes or until shrimp turn rosy pink. Remove shrimp from pan; set aside.

Add bell peppers and broccoli to pan; cook over high heat for 1 minute. Add water; cover and reduce heat to medium. Cook 4 to 5 minutes or until vegetables are tender.

Uncover pan and return heat to high. Add shrimp and marmalade mixture. Cook for another 2 minutes until sauce is thickened and shrimp are completely cooked. Season with salt and freshly ground pepper, if desired. Stir in green onions. Serve with hot cooked rice.

MANDARIN SHRIMP AND VEGETABLE STIR-FRY

Apricot-Glazed Spareribs

6 servings

6 POUNDS PORK SPARERIBS, CUT
    INTO 2-RIB PORTIONS
4 CLOVES GARLIC, CRUSHED
    WATER
1 CUP (12-OUNCE JAR) **SMUCKER'S**
    APRICOT PRESERVES
¼ CUP CHOPPED ONION
¼ CUP KETCHUP
2 TABLESPOONS FIRMLY PACKED
    BROWN SUGAR
1 TABLESPOON OIL
1 TEASPOON SOY SAUCE
1 TEASPOON GINGER
½ TEASPOON SALT

Early in day or day ahead:
In very large saucepot or Dutch oven, combine pork spareribs and garlic; cover with water. Over high heat, heat to boiling. Reduce heat to low; cover and simmer 1 hour or until spareribs are fork-tender. Remove ribs to platter; cover and refrigerate.

Meanwhile, prepare apricot glaze: combine preserves, onion, ketchup, brown sugar, oil, soy sauce, ginger and salt in small saucepan; mix well. Heat to boiling; boil 1 minute. Cover and refrigerate apricot glaze.

About 1 hour before serving: heat grill. When ready to barbecue, place cooked spareribs on grill over medium heat. Cook 12 to 15 minutes or until heated through, turning spareribs often. Brush occasionally with apricot glaze during last 10 minutes of cooking.

Note: The precooked spareribs can be broiled in the oven. Place spareribs on broiler pan; brush with some apricot glaze. Broil about 7 to 9 inches from heat for 7 to 8 minutes, brushing with apricot glaze halfway through cooking time. Turn ribs, brush with apricot glaze and broil for 5 to 6 minutes, brushing with apricot glaze halfway through cooking time.

Caribbean Baked Chicken Breasts with Banana Apricot Stuffing

4 servings

- 1 SMALL BANANA, FINELY CHOPPED
- 1/4 CUP **SMUCKER'S** APRICOT PRESERVES
- 1/4 TEASPOON FRESHLY GROUND PEPPER
- 4 BONELESS SKINLESS CHICKEN BREASTS
- 1/4 CUP LITE SOY SAUCE
- 1 TEASPOON HOT PEPPER SAUCE
- 1 TEASPOON CHOPPED GARLIC
  JUICE OF 1 LEMON (ABOUT 1/3 CUP)
- 1 CUP DRY BREAD CRUMBS
  SALT AND PEPPER
- 2 TEASPOONS OIL OR NONSTICK COOKING SPRAY

Combine banana, preserves and pepper; mix well. Make small slit in side of each chicken breast, 2/3 of the way through and large enough to hold two tablespoons of stuffing. Stuff breasts with banana mixture. Close pockets securely with toothpicks.

Combine soy sauce, hot pepper sauce, garlic and lemon juice; mix well. Season bread crumbs with salt and pepper. One at a time, dip chicken breasts in soy sauce mixture, then dredge in bread crumbs.

Add oil to nonstick skillet or coat with nonstick cooking spray; heat over medium heat until hot. Add chicken; cook for 4 minutes or until lightly browned, turning once. Place on baking sheet.

Bake at 375° for 20 minutes or until chicken breasts are firm and thoroughly cooked. Discard toothpicks and serve immediately.

Apricot-Glazed Hens with Wild Rice Stuffing

4 servings

¼ CUP BUTTER OR MARGARINE
½ CUP CHOPPED ONIONS
¾ CUP DICED CELERY
1 (6-OUNCE) PACKAGE LONG GRAIN AND WILD RICE MIX
2½ CUPS WATER
1 CUP (12-OUNCE JAR) **SMUCKER'S** APRICOT PRESERVES
2 TABLESPOONS CHOPPED PARSLEY
⅓ CUP CHOPPED TOASTED PECANS
4 CORNISH GAME HENS (ABOUT 22 OUNCES EACH)
SALT AND PEPPER
LEMON SLICES AND CELERY LEAVES

Melt butter in large saucepan; remove 2 tablespoons melted butter and set aside. Add onions and celery to saucepan. Sauté over medium heat, stirring frequently, until onions begin to turn golden. Add rice mix and water; cover and cook according to package directions. Add ¼ cup of the apricot preserves, parsley and pecans. Use mixture to stuff hens, or serve as a side dish in a 3 to 4 cup casserole dish.

Fill hens with stuffing; secure cavities with poultry pins or toothpicks. Brush hens with reserved butter; sprinkle lightly with salt and pepper.

Roast at 350° for 70 to 75 minutes or until legs of hens can be moved easily up and down. Baste hens with remaining apricot preserves during last 15 minutes of roasting.

To serve, remove poultry pins from hens; place hens on large serving platter. Garnish with lemon slices and celery leaves. Serve apricot drippings from hens as sauce in small dish; thin with water and heat, if necessary.

APRICOT-GLAZED HENS WITH WILD RICE STUFFING

63

Raspberry-Glazed Turkey

4 to 6 servings

1/2 CUP **SMUCKER'S** SEEDLESS RED RASPBERRY JAM

6 TABLESPOONS RASPBERRY VINEGAR

1/4 CUP DIJON MUSTARD

4 SMALL TURKEY BREAST TENDERLOINS

In large saucepan, stir together jam, vinegar and mustard. Bring to a boil over high heat; cook and stir 3 minutes. Reserve about 1/2 cup of the glaze; coat turkey with some of the remaining glaze.

Set turkey on rack in broiler pan. Broil about 4 inches from heat for 15 to 20 minutes or until no longer pink in center, turning and basting once with remaining glaze.

Slice turkey crosswise. Serve with reserved glaze.

RASPBERRY-GLAZED TURKEY, APRICOT CARROTS PAGE 51

Baked Ham with Apple-Raspberry Sauce

8 to 10 servings

1 (3-POUND) CANNED HAM
1 CUP CHOPPED APPLES
½ CUP **SMUCKER'S** RED RASPBERRY PRESERVES
½ CUP **SMUCKER'S** APPLE JELLY
¾ CUP APPLE CIDER
1 TABLESPOON CIDER VINEGAR
2 TABLESPOONS CORNSTARCH
ENDIVE OR PARSLEY SPRIGS
WHOLE CRABAPPLES

Bake ham according to package directions.

Mix chopped apples, preserves and jelly in medium saucepan. Combine cider, vinegar and cornstarch; stir into saucepan. Heat to boiling; boil, stirring constantly, until thickened, about 1 minute.

Slice ham and arrange on platter; garnish with endive and crabapples. Serve with sauce.

Grilled Sausage with Apricot-Mustard Glaze

4 servings

½ CUP **SMUCKER'S** APRICOT PRESERVES
½ CUP DIJON-STYLE MUSTARD
1 POUND SMOKED PORK SAUSAGE
4 FRENCH SANDWICH ROLLS

Combine preserves and mustard; blend well. Set aside.

Cut pork sausage into 2-inch pieces and place on baking sheet. Grill or broil for 4 minutes; turn and cook for another 4 minutes.

Remove baking sheet from the heat and dip each piece in apricot-mustard glaze. Return to broiler or grill and cook for 2 more minutes or until lightly browned. Divide among sandwich rolls; serve with additional apricot-mustard glaze on the side.

Pork Chops and Yams

4 servings

4   PORK CHOPS (1/2-INCH THICK)
2   TABLESPOONS OIL
2   (16-OUNCE) CANS YAMS, DRAINED
1/2 LARGE GREEN BELL PEPPER,
     CUT INTO STRIPS
2   TABLESPOONS MINCED ONION
3/4 CUP **SMUCKER'S** SWEET ORANGE
     MARMALADE OR APRICOT
     PRESERVES

Brown pork chops in oil over medium heat.

Place yams in 1 1/2-quart casserole. Stir in green pepper, onions and marmalade. Layer pork chops over yam mixture. Cover and bake at 350° for 30 minutes or until pork chops are tender.

Grilled Apricot-Ginger Turkey

4 servings

1/2 CUP **SMUCKER'S**
     APRICOT PRESERVES
1/2 TEASPOON GINGER
1/4 TEASPOON PEPPER
4   TURKEY STEAKS
     (1/2 POUND EACH)
2   TABLESPOONS OIL

Combine preserves, ginger and pepper; mix well.

Brush turkey with oil; place on grill about 4 inches from heat. Cook for 6 to 8 minutes, turning once and brushing frequently with preserves mixture.

Peppered Steaks with Blackberry Sauce

4 servings

STEAKS
- 1/3 CUP LEMON JUICE
- 1/3 CUP OIL
- 1/4 CUP CHOPPED ONION
- 2 CLOVES GARLIC, CRUSHED
- 4 (4 TO 6-OUNCE) BEEF TENDERLOIN OR EYE OF ROUND STEAKS, TRIMMED OF FAT
- 1 TABLESPOON COARSE GROUND PEPPER

BLACKBERRY SAUCE
- 1/2 CUP **SMUCKER'S** SEEDLESS BLACKBERRY JAM
- 1/4 CUP RED WINE VINEGAR
- 1/4 TEASPOON ONION POWDER
- 1/4 CUP FRESH OR FROZEN BLACKBERRIES, THAWED

Combine lemon juice, oil, onion and garlic in large resealable plastic bag; mix well. Place steaks in marinade, seal and refrigerate 6 to 24 hours, turning bag occasionally. When ready to cook, rub pepper around outside edges of each steak.

Heat grill. In small saucepan, combine jam, vinegar and onion powder. Cook over medium heat until jam is melted, stirring constantly. Remove from heat.

Oil grill rack. Place steaks on gas grill over medium heat or on charcoal grill 4 to 6 inches from medium-high coals. Cook 8 to 12 minutes or until desired doneness, turning once halfway through cooking. To serve, spread steaks with blackberry sauce; top with fresh berries.

Note: Steaks can be cooked in the broiler. Place on oiled broiler pan. Broil 4 to 6 inches from heat for 7 to 10 minutes or until desired doneness, turning once halfway through cooking.

PEPPERED STEAKS WITH BLACKBERRY SAUCE

Sautéed Swordfish with Cherry Salsa

6 servings

SALSA

½	CUP	**SMUCKER'S** CHERRY PRESERVES
½	CUP	COARSELY CHOPPED ONIONS
1	CUP	COARSELY CHOPPED RED BELL PEPPERS
1	CUP	COARSELY CHOPPED GREEN BELL PEPPERS
2	CUPS	COARSELY CHOPPED FRESH TOMATOES
¼	CUP	MINCED JALAPEÑO OR OTHER HOT CHILE PEPPERS
1	TEASPOON	HOT PEPPER SAUCE
½	TEASPOON	SALT

SWORDFISH

3 TO 4 TABLESPOONS OIL

1 ½ POUNDS FRESH SWORDFISH, CUT INTO 6 PORTIONS ABOUT 1 INCH THICK

SALT AND PEPPER

Combine all salsa ingredients in food processor; blend for 5 to 10 seconds or until salsa is slightly chunky. Season with pepper, additional hot pepper sauce and/or additional salt, if desired.

Heat oil in nonstick skillet over medium-high heat. Lightly season swordfish with salt and pepper; place in skillet.

Cook on one side for 5 to 7 minutes; turn and cook 8 minutes or longer, until done. Swordfish is done when slightly firm to the touch.

Place swordfish on 6 individual serving plates; top each with a few tablespoons of salsa.

Garnish with fresh lemon slices, if desired.

Sweet and Sour Chicken Stir-Fry

4 servings

½ CUP **SMUCKER'S** LOW SUGAR
   APRICOT PRESERVES
1 TABLESPOON VINEGAR
1 TEASPOON GARLIC SALT
1 TEASPOON GINGER
1 TEASPOON SOY SAUCE
⅛ TEASPOON CRUSHED
   RED PEPPER FLAKES
2 MEDIUM ZUCCHINI
2 WHOLE LARGE CHICKEN BREASTS,
   SKINNED, BONED AND CUT INTO
   1-INCH CUBES
¼ CUP OIL
½ POUND SMALL MUSHROOMS,
   SLICED
½ TEASPOON SALT
1 (6-OUNCE) PACKAGE FROZEN
   PEA PODS, THAWED
   HOT COOKED RICE, IF DESIRED

Combine preserves, vinegar, garlic salt, ginger, soy sauce and crushed red pepper flakes; stir until well blended. Set aside.

Halve zucchini lengthwise. Cut into ¼-inch slices; set aside. Heat 2 tablespoons oil in wok or Dutch oven over high heat; stir-fry chicken until tender and browned. Add remaining oil, zucchini, mushrooms and salt to chicken. Stir-fry until zucchini is crisp-tender. Add pea pods and apricot sauce; toss gently to mix well and heat through. Serve with hot cooked rice.

Curried Meatballs

6 servings

1½ POUNDS GROUND BEEF
1 CUP FRESH BREAD CRUMBS
1 CUP TOMATO JUICE
1½ TEASPOONS SALT
⅛ TEASPOON PEPPER
¼ CUP ALL-PURPOSE FLOUR
2 TABLESPOONS BUTTER
   OR MARGARINE
2 MEDIUM ONIONS, SLICED
1 TEASPOON CURRY POWDER
½ CUP **SMUCKER'S**
   APPLE JELLY
1 CUP BEEF BROTH OR BOUILLON
   HOT COOKED RICE

Combine ground beef, bread crumbs, ½ cup of the tomato juice, salt and pepper. Shape into 36 small balls, 1¼ to 1½ inches in diameter; roll in flour to coat all sides. Melt butter in large skillet; add meatballs and brown on all sides. Remove meatballs and set aside.

Remove all but 2 tablespoons of drippings from skillet. Add onions and curry powder to remaining drippings in skillet; cook, stirring frequently, just until onions are soft. Add jelly, beef broth and remaining ½ cup tomato juice. Bring to a boil. Return meatballs to skillet. Cover and simmer 20 minutes, stirring often. Serve with hot cooked rice.

Peachy Pork Roast

8 to 10 servings

1 (3 TO 4-POUND) ROLLED
   BONELESS PORK LOIN ROAST
1 CUP (12-OUNCE JAR) **SMUCKER'S**
   CURRANT JELLY
½ CUP **SMUCKER'S**
   PEACH PRESERVES
   FRESH PEACH SLICES AND
   CURRANTS FOR GARNISH,
   IF DESIRED

Insert meat thermometer into one end of roast. Bake at 325° for 30 to 40 minutes or until browned. Turn roast and bake an additional 30 minutes to brown the bottom. Turn roast again and drain off drippings.

In saucepan over medium heat, melt currant jelly and peach preserves. Brush roast generously with sauce.

Continue baking until meat thermometer reads 160°, about 15 minutes, basting occasionally with sauce.

Remove roast from oven. Garnish with peach slices and currants. Serve with remaining sauce.

Note: Canned, sliced peaches can be substituted for fresh peaches.

PEACHY PORK ROAST

Saucy Chicken Kiev Olé

8 servings

1/3 CUP BUTTER OR MARGARINE, SOFTENED

1 (1.24 TO 1.31-OUNCE) PACKAGE TACO SEASONING MIX

1 CUP (4 OUNCES) SHREDDED CHEDDAR CHEESE

4 WHOLE CHICKEN BREASTS, HALVED, SKINNED AND BONED

1 CUP (12-OUNCE JAR) **SMUCKER'S** TOMATO PRESERVES*

1 (8-OUNCE) JAR TACO SAUCE

1/2 CUP PITTED RIPE OLIVES, SLICED

2 CUPS SHREDDED ICEBERG LETTUCE

2 MEDIUM TOMATOES, CUT INTO WEDGES

Combine butter, taco seasoning mix and 1/4 cup of the cheese until well blended. Place each chicken breast in small plastic bag. With rolling pin, pound chicken breasts to 1/4-inch thickness; discard bag. Place equal amounts of butter mixture in centers of flattened chicken. Fold sides over center; secure with toothpicks. Place chicken, smooth side up, in 12x8-inch baking dish.

Mix tomato preserves and taco sauce. Set aside 1 cup sauce mixture; pour remaining mixture over chicken. Cover with foil.

Bake at 350° for 25 minutes. Remove foil; top chicken with remaining 3/4 cup cheese and olives. Bake uncovered for an additional 5 minutes or until cheese is melted and bubbly.

To serve, arrange lettuce on serving platter. Top with chicken; garnish with tomato wedges. Serve with reserved sauce mixture.

Note: *If tomato preserves are not available, substitute 1 cup (12-ounce jar) of Smucker's Apple Jelly PLUS a 6-ounce can of tomato paste. Combine jelly, tomato paste and taco sauce in small saucepan; stir over low heat until jelly melts. Reserve 1 cup of mixture and continue as directed.

Mediterranean Chicken

6 servings

1 TEASPOON OIL

4 BONELESS SKINLESS CHICKEN BREASTS, CUBED

2 (10.75-OUNCE) JARS **LOST ACRES COUNTRY SIDES** MEDITERRANEAN RELISH

¼ CUP **SMUCKER'S** SWEET ORANGE MARMALADE

¼ CUP WATER

½ CUP GRATED PARMESAN CHEESE PASTA OR RICE, COOKED

Brown chicken in oil; drain.

Combine chicken, relish, orange marmalade and water; mix well. Place in 2-quart casserole dish; top with cheese.

Bake at 350° for 30 minutes or until hot and bubbly. Serve over hot cooked pasta or rice.

Note: A packaged rice pilaf mix would be a quick, delicious choice to accompany this recipe.

Karen Befus
Sales Assistant
JMS Specialty Foods
Ripon, Wisconsin
Employee since 1994

"In this recipe, marmalade adds just enough sweetness
to enhance the taste of the chicken."

Carnival Pork Stew

8 servings

3 POUNDS LEAN BONELESS PORK LOIN, CUT INTO 2-INCH PIECES

SALT AND FRESH GROUND PEPPER

2 TABLESPOONS OIL

8 OUNCES SMOKED HAM, CUT INTO ½-INCH CHUNKS

2 MEDIUM ONIONS, CHOPPED

2 STALKS CELERY, CHOPPED

2 GREEN BELL PEPPERS, CHOPPED

6 CLOVES GARLIC, MINCED

½ TEASPOON DRIED THYME

1 (28-OUNCE) CAN WHOLE TOMATOES, UNDRAINED, CUT UP

¾ CUP **SMUCKER'S** PEACH PRESERVES

1 CUP WATER

1 TABLESPOON HOT PEPPER SAUCE

½ CUP CHOPPED FRESH PARSLEY

½ CUP CHOPPED GREEN ONIONS

1 CUP UNCOOKED LONG-GRAIN RICE

Sprinkle pork with salt and pepper. Heat oil in large Dutch oven. Add pork; cook 5 to 8 minutes or until well browned. Remove pork with slotted spoon; set aside.

Add ham, onions, celery, green peppers, garlic and thyme. Cook over medium-high heat until vegetables are wilted, about 6 minutes. Add browned pork, tomatoes, preserves, water and hot pepper sauce. Cover and simmer for 45 minutes.

Add parsley, green onions and rice; stir to blend well. Cover and simmer 20 to 25 minutes or until rice is tender. Add salt and pepper to taste.

Grilled Spicy Red Snapper with Jamaican Mango and Peach Relish

4 servings

RELISH

1/2 CUP **SMUCKER'S** PEACH PRESERVES

JUICE OF 1 LEMON (ABOUT 1/3 CUP)

1 SMALL ONION, FINELY CHOPPED

1 TEASPOON MINCED GARLIC

1/4 TEASPOON ALLSPICE

1/4 TEASPOON SALT

1/4 TEASPOON FRESHLY GROUND PEPPER

1 LARGE RIPE MANGO, PEELED AND FINELY CHOPPED

RED SNAPPER

1 POUND RED SNAPPER OR SWORDFISH FILLETS, CUT INTO 4 PORTIONS

JUICE OF 1 LIME (ABOUT 1/3 CUP)

1/2 TEASPOON FINELY CHOPPED HOT CHILI PEPPER, OR TO TASTE

2 TABLESPOONS CHOPPED FRESH PARSLEY, CHIVES OR THYME—OR A COMBINATION OF ALL THREE

SALT AND PEPPER

2 TABLESPOONS OIL

LEMON WEDGES, IF DESIRED

Combine all relish ingredients except mango; mix well. Fold in mango. Cover and chill before serving.

Using sharp knife, lightly score one side of each fish fillet with 3 to 4 X's. Place fillets in shallow dish and rub with lime juice, hot pepper, herbs, salt and pepper. Refrigerate at least 1 hour or overnight.

When ready to cook, heat grill or broiler. Lightly oil fillets. Place on grill or broiler pan. Cook fish for 4 to 6 minutes; turn and cook for 3 to 5 minutes or until the fish is slightly firm to the touch. Serve with Jamaican mango and peach relish; garnish with lemon wedges, if desired.

GRILLED SPICY RED SNAPPER WITH JAMAICAN MANGO AND PEACH RELISH

Saucy Chicken

8 servings

2 POUNDS CHICKEN BREASTS
1 (8-OUNCE) BOTTLE RUSSIAN
   OR FRENCH SALAD DRESSING
1 (1.25-OUNCE) ENVELOPE ONION
   SOUP MIX (DRY)
1 CUP (12-OUNCE JAR) **SMUCKER'S**
   APRICOT PRESERVES
   HOT COOKED RICE

Place chicken skin-side-up in 13x9-inch baking pan. Combine dressing, soup mix and preserves; mix well. Pour over chicken.

Bake at 350° for 1 hour or until chicken is fork-tender and juices run clear; halfway through cooking time, spoon sauce over breasts. Serve over hot cooked rice.

Cranberry Orange Game Hens with Vegetable Stuffing

4 servings

GAME HENS
4 SMALL CORNISH GAME HENS
   (16 OUNCES EACH)
1 CARROT, FINELY DICED
1 STALK CELERY, FINELY DICED
2 CUPS BREAD STUFFING MIX
1 TEASPOON POULTRY SEASONING
1 CUP CHICKEN STOCK OR BROTH
   SALT AND PEPPER

SAUCE
1 CUP FRESH OR FROZEN
   CRANBERRIES, CHOPPED
1 CUP (12-OUNCE JAR) **SMUCKER'S**
   SWEET ORANGE MARMALADE
¼ CUP WATER
1 TEASPOON LEMON JUICE
   LEMON WEDGES, IF DESIRED

Remove as much fat as possible from game hens. Combine carrots, celery, stuffing mix, poultry seasoning and chicken stock. Season with salt and pepper. Fill cavity of each hen with stuffing; place on roasting pan. Bake at 400° for 45 minutes.

Meanwhile, prepare sauce. In medium saucepan, combine all sauce ingredients. Cook over medium-high heat for 5 to 8 minutes until cranberries have released their juice. Set aside.

Remove game hens from oven. Spread sauce over top and sides of hens. Reserve any extra sauce to serve later with hens. Return hens to oven and finish baking for another 10 to 15 minutes.

To serve, place game hens on 4 serving plates. Spoon some stuffing onto each plate. Spoon additional sauce onto hens. Serve each garnished with a wedge of fresh lemon.

Baked Fish

4 servings

1 1/2 POUNDS FIRM-FLESHED FISH FILLETS (SUCH AS SWORDFISH, TUNA OR SEABASS), CUT INTO SERVING-SIZED PIECES
1/2 CUP **SMUCKER'S** PLUM PRESERVES
1 TABLESPOON SOY SAUCE
1 TEASPOON CORNSTARCH
1/2 TEASPOON GINGER
2 CLOVES GARLIC, FINELY MINCED
SALT AND PEPPER

PLUM SAUCE

1/2 CUP **SMUCKER'S** PLUM PRESERVES
1 CLOVE GARLIC, FINELY MINCED
2 TEASPOONS SOY SAUCE
1/4 TEASPOON PEPPER

Rinse fish and pat dry. Place in 9-inch baking dish coated with nonstick cooking spray.

Combine preserves, soy sauce, cornstarch, ginger, garlic, and salt and pepper. Mix well. Pour over fish. Bake, uncovered, at 350° for 20 minutes or until the thickest pieces of fish flake with a fork. Do not overbake.

Meanwhile, in small saucepan, combine all ingredients for plum sauce and cook over low heat, stirring occasionally for 3 minutes. Serve with fish.

Glazed Pork Chops

4 to 6 servings

6 PORK LOIN OR RIB CHOPS, 3/4 INCH THICK
1 CUP (12-OUNCE JAR) **SMUCKER'S** BLACKBERRY JAM
3/4 CUP KETCHUP
1/4 CUP STEAK SAUCE
1 TEASPOON DRY MUSTARD
1 CLOVE GARLIC, MINCED

Broil pork chops 3 to 5 inches from heat for 5 minutes. Turn; broil 5 minutes longer.

Meanwhile, in small saucepan, combine remaining ingredients. Heat to boiling; simmer over low heat for 10 minutes.

Brush pork with sauce. Continue broiling, turning and brushing with sauce, 5 to 10 minutes longer, or until pork is no longer pink in center. Bring remaining sauce to a boil; serve with pork chops.

CRÊPES À L'ORANGE WITH RASPBERRY-ORANGE CREAM FILLING PAGE 82

Desserts

CRÊPES À L'ORANGE WITH RASPBERRY-ORANGE CREAM FILLING

Crêpes à l'Orange with Raspberry-Orange Cream Filling

4 servings

CRÊPES
1/2 CUP ALL-PURPOSE FLOUR
2 TABLESPOONS SUGAR
1 TABLESPOON GRATED ORANGE PEEL
1/8 TEASPOON SALT
1 CUP MILK
3 EGGS, BEATEN
2 TABLESPOONS OIL

FILLING
2 CUPS HEAVY CREAM
1/4 CUP **SMUCKER'S** SEEDLESS RED RASPBERRY JAM
1/4 CUP **SMUCKER'S** SWEET ORANGE MARMALADE
1 CUP FRESH RASPBERRIES

ORANGE YOGURT SAUCE
1 CUP LOW-FAT PLAIN YOGURT
1/4 CUP **SMUCKER'S** SWEET ORANGE MARMALADE
1/2 CUP ORANGE JUICE

To make crêpes, combine flour, sugar, orange peel and salt. Add milk gradually and stir until mixture is free of lumps. Add eggs and oil; blend well. Lightly butter small skillet or crêpe pan. Pour 1/4 cup batter into hot skillet; tilt to spread batter over bottom. Cook over medium heat until top of crêpe is covered with bubbles and edges are beginning to brown. Turn; cook underside. Repeat using remaining batter. Stack crêpes between sheets of waxed paper.

To make filling, whip heavy cream. Fold in jam, marmalade and 1/2 cup of the raspberries. To make sauce, combine all sauce ingredients; stir well.

To assemble, lay crêpes on flat surface; top with filling. Roll up crêpes firmly and cut in half. Pour orange yogurt sauce onto 4 plates. Place 3 crêpe halves on each plate pointing to the center. Decorate with remaining raspberries.

Double Apple Turnovers

6 turnovers

1/2 CUP **SMUCKER'S** CIDER APPLE BUTTER

1/2 CUP APPLE CIDER OR JUICE

1/2 TEASPOON CINNAMON

1 ORANGE PEEL, GRATED*

1/4 CUP GOLDEN RAISINS

4 LARGE FIRM APPLES, PEELED, CORED AND CHOPPED

1 PACKAGE FROZEN FILO (PHYLLO) DOUGH

NONSTICK COOKING SPRAY

SUGAR

In large saucepan, combine apple butter, cider, cinnamon and grated orange peel; simmer for 5 minutes. Add raisins and simmer for 2 minutes more. Add apples and cook over medium heat for about 10 minutes or until apples begin to soften and most of liquid evaporates. Cool in refrigerator.

Unwrap filo dough but keep covered with damp cloth. Remove 1 sheet of dough; spray with nonstick cooking spray. Top with second sheet of dough; spray with nonstick cooking spray. Spoon about 1/3 cup of apple filling on lower right corner of the dough. Fold dough over filling to form a large rectangle. Then fold turnover as if it were a flag, making a triangular packet with each turn. Repeat this process until all turnovers are made.

Place finished turnovers on baking sheet; sprinkle with sugar. Bake at 375° for about 25 minutes or until golden brown.

Note: *Grate orange part of peel only, not bitter white part.

Vanilla Mousse in Fluted Chocolate Cups

24 servings

3/4 CUP (7.25 OUNCE BOTTLE) **SMUCKER'S MAGIC SHELL** CHOCOLATE OR CHOCOLATE FUDGE ICE CREAM TOPPING

1 PACKAGE (24) FOIL BAKING CUPS (1 3/4-INCH IN DIAMETER)

2/3 CUP EVAPORATED MILK, THOROUGHLY CHILLED

1 EGG

1/4 CUP SUGAR

SALT

1 TEASPOON VANILLA

24 MINT LEAVES, IF DESIRED

24 MARASCHINO CHERRY SLICES, IF DESIRED

Pour Magic Shell into small bowl. With small, dry pastry brush, thinly and evenly coat insides of baking cups with Magic Shell. Chill in freezer for several minutes. Coat and freeze each cup at least 3 more times. Store cups in freezer.

Whip evaporated milk until stiff. Beat in egg, sugar, a pinch of salt and vanilla. Spoon or pipe mousse into fluted chocolate cups. Freeze until firm. Before serving, carefully remove foil and garnish each cup with 1 mint leaf and 1 maraschino cherry slice. For extended storage, cover tops of cups lightly with plastic wrap and store in freezer up to 1 week.

PEACH COBBLER WITH VANILLA CREAM

Peach Cobbler with Vanilla Cream

6 to 8 servings

1/3 CUP **SMUCKER'S** PEACH PRESERVES
1/4 CUP PLUS 2 TEASPOONS SUGAR
1 TABLESPOON CORNSTARCH
1/4 TEASPOON PLUS 1/8 TEASPOON NUTMEG
2 (16-OUNCE) PACKAGES FROZEN UNSWEETENED SLICED PEACHES, THAWED AND WELL DRAINED
1 TEASPOON LEMON JUICE
1/2 TEASPOON VANILLA
1 (7.5-OUNCE) PACKAGE REFRIGERATED BUTTERMILK BISCUITS
1 TABLESPOON BUTTER OR MARGARINE, MELTED

VANILLA CREAM
1 CUP (1/2 PINT) WHIPPING CREAM
1 TABLESPOON SUGAR
2 TEASPOONS VANILLA

In large saucepan, combine peach preserves, 1/4 cup of the sugar, cornstarch and 1/4 teaspoon of the nutmeg. Stir in peach slices and lemon juice. Cook over medium-high heat, stirring frequently, for about 5 minutes or until mixture thickens and boils. Boil, stirring constantly, for 1 minute. Stir in vanilla. Pour fruit mixture into ungreased shallow 2-quart casserole.

Combine remaining 2 teaspoons sugar and 1/8 teaspoon nutmeg; set aside. Working quickly, separate buttermilk biscuits and arrange in single layer on top of hot fruit.

Bake at 450° for 8 to 10 minutes or until biscuits are golden brown and fruit mixture is bubbling. Immediately brush biscuits with melted butter; sprinkle with sugar-nutmeg mixture. Prepare vanilla cream: combine whipping cream, sugar and vanilla; stir until blended. Serve cobbler warm with vanilla cream.

Note: To prevent sogginess, fruit mixture should be boiling hot when topped with uncooked biscuits.

Fudgy Peanut Butter Cake

12 to 15 servings

- 1 (18.25-OUNCE) BOX CHOCOLATE FUDGE CAKE MIX
- 2 EGGS
- 1 1/2 CUPS WATER
- 1 (16-OUNCE) PACKAGE CHOCOLATE FUDGE FROSTING MIX
- 1 1/4 CUPS **SMUCKER'S** CHUNKY NATURAL PEANUT BUTTER OR **LAURA SCUDDER'S** NUTTY OLD-FASHIONED PEANUT BUTTER
- 2/3 CUP WATER

Grease and flour 10-inch tube pan. In large bowl, blend cake mix, eggs and 1 1/2 cups water until moistened; mix as directed on cake package. Pour batter into pan.

In medium bowl, combine frosting mix, peanut butter and 2/3 cup water; blend until smooth. Spoon over batter in pan.

Bake at 350° for 35 to 45 minutes or until top springs back when touched lightly in center. Cool upright in pan 1 hour; remove from pan. Cool completely.

Cheesecake Sensation

12 to 14 servings

- 1/4 CUP GRAHAM CRACKER CRUMBS
- 4 (8-OUNCE) PACKAGES CREAM CHEESE, SOFTENED
- 4 EGGS
- 1 3/4 CUPS SUGAR
- 2 TABLESPOONS LEMON JUICE
- 2 TABLESPOONS GRATED LEMON PEEL
- 1 TEASPOON VANILLA
- 1/2 CUP **SMUCKER'S** NATURAL APRICOT SYRUP
- 1/2 CUP **SMUCKER'S** STRAWBERRY PRESERVES

Butter inside of straight-side casserole or soufflé dish 8 inches wide and 3 inches deep. Do not use a springform pan. Sprinkle with graham cracker crumbs and shake around bottom and sides until coated. Set aside.

Combine cream cheese, eggs, sugar, lemon juice, lemon peel and vanilla; beat at low speed and, as ingredients blend, increase speed to high, scraping bowl several times. Continue beating until thoroughly blended and smooth. Pour batter into prepared dish; shake gently to level mixture. Set dish inside slightly wider pan; add boiling water to larger pan to a depth of about 1/2 inch. Do not let edge of cheesecake dish touch rim of larger pan.

Bake at 325° for 1 1/2 to 2 hours or until set. Turn off oven; let cake sit in oven 20 minutes longer. Lift cake dish out of larger pan and place on wire rack. Cool about 2 hours or until cake reaches room temperature.

Invert plate over the cheesecake and carefully turn upside down so cake comes out crumb side up. Slowly spoon syrup over cake. Just before serving, spoon preserves in a narrow ring around outer rim of cake.

Ice Cream Cookie Dessert

12 to 16 servings

1 (1 1/4-POUND) PACKAGE CHOCOLATE SANDWICH COOKIES
1 STACK (18 COOKIES) CHOCOLATE FUDGE MINT COOKIES
1/2 GALLON VANILLA OR MINT CHOCOLATE CHIP ICE CREAM, SOFTENED
2 CUPS (TWO 12-OUNCE JARS) **SMUCKER'S** HOT FUDGE TOPPING
1 (12-OUNCE) CARTON WHIPPED TOPPING, THAWED

Crush cookies until fine. Reserve 1 cup of crumbs for topping. Press remaining cookie crumbs in 13x9-inch pan. Spoon ice cream on top of crumbs and freeze.

Heat hot fudge topping as directed on jar; spread over ice cream. Freeze for 1 hour.

Spread with whipped topping; top with reserved cookie crumbs. Freeze until ready to serve.

Old-Fashioned Caramel Pie

6 to 8 servings

3 LARGE EGGS
1 CUP (12-OUNCE JAR) **SMUCKER'S** CARAMEL TOPPING
1/2 CUP SUGAR
1/2 CUP MILK
1 CUP QUICK-COOKING OR OLD-FASHIONED OATS
1/4 CUP BUTTER, MELTED
1/8 TEASPOON SALT
1 TEASPOON VANILLA
1 9-INCH PIE SHELL, BAKED

In large bowl, beat eggs. Add remaining ingredients; blend well. Pour into baked pie shell.

Bake at 350° for 1 hour or until set.

Linzer Torte

10 servings

- 1 CUP SLIVERED ALMONDS
- 1 ¼ CUPS UNSIFTED ALL-PURPOSE FLOUR
- ¼ CUP SUGAR
- 2 EGGS
- ½ CUP BUTTER OR MARGARINE, SOFTENED
- 1 TABLESPOON GRATED LEMON PEEL
- ½ TEASPOON ALMOND EXTRACT
- ¾ CUP **SMUCKER'S** APRICOT PRESERVES
- ¼ CUP **SMUCKER'S** RED RASPBERRY PRESERVES

Finely chop almonds in food processor or blender. Lightly spoon flour into measuring cup; level off. In food processor or large bowl of electric mixer, stir together almonds, flour and sugar.

Separate one egg, set white aside. Add egg yolk, remaining whole egg, butter, lemon peel and almond extract to flour mixture. Process or mix until dough forms a ball.

Remove scant ⅓ of dough; flatten, wrap and refrigerate for at least ½ hour or until manageable.

Grease 9-inch round tart pan with removable bottom. Press remaining dough in bottom and about ½ inch up sides of pan. Spread ½ cup of the apricot preserves evenly over dough.

Remove refrigerated dough. On floured surface or between sheets of waxed paper, roll into 9½ x 5-inch rectangle. Cut into ten (½-inch-wide) strips. Place one strip across center of torte. Place second strip on each side, about 2 inches in from edge. Repeat in other

direction. Now place a strip between center and edge strips in each direction. Press strips to edge. Trim off evenly with knife or pastry wheel.

Brush strips with reserved egg white. Spoon remaining apricot preserves and raspberry preserves in alternate spaces between strips.

LINZER TORTE

Bake at 350° for 30 minutes or until crust is golden brown. Cool 10 minutes. Remove sides of pan. Serve warm or cool. Keeps for up to 1 week, tightly covered.

Note: If crust bubbles up during baking, poke with wooden pick to break bubbles.

THUMBPRINT COOKIES

Thumbprint Cookies

2½ dozen cookies

1 CUP BUTTER OR MARGARINE
¼ CUP SUGAR
1 TEASPOON ALMOND EXTRACT
2 CUPS ALL-PURPOSE FLOUR
½ TEASPOON SALT
1 CUP FINELY CHOPPED NUTS,
   IF DESIRED
   SMUCKER'S PRESERVES
   OR JAMS (ANY FLAVOR)

Combine butter and sugar; beat until light and fluffy. Blend in almond extract. Add flour and salt; mix well.

Shape level tablespoonfuls of dough into balls; roll in nuts. Place on ungreased cookie sheets; flatten slightly. Indent centers; fill with preserves or jams.

Bake at 400° for 10 to 12 minutes or just until lightly browned.

CHEWY RED RASPBERRY BARS,
ORANGE MARMALADE COOKIES PAGE 102

Chewy
Red Raspberry Bars

12 bars

1/2 CUP BUTTER OR MARGARINE,
    ROOM TEMPERATURE
  1 CUP FIRMLY PACKED LIGHT BROWN
    SUGAR
1/2 TEASPOON ALMOND EXTRACT
  1 CUP ALL-PURPOSE FLOUR
  1 TEASPOON BAKING POWDER
  1 CUP QUICK-COOKING OR
    OLD-FASHIONED OATS
1/2 CUP **SMUCKER'S** RED RASPBERRY
    PRESERVES

Combine butter and brown sugar; beat until fluffy. Beat in almond extract. Mix in flour, baking powder and oats until crumbly. Reserve 1/4 cup mixture; pat remaining mixture in bottom of greased 8-inch square baking pan. Dot preserves over crumb mixture in pan; sprinkle with reserved crumb mixture.

Bake at 350° for 30 to 40 minutes or until brown. Cool on wire rack. Cut into bars.

Apple Butter Anniversary Cake

16 servings

CAKE

- 1 (18.25-OUNCE) PACKAGE YELLOW CAKE MIX
- 1 CUP (11-OUNCE JAR) **SMUCKER'S** CIDER APPLE BUTTER
- 1/3 CUP SOUR CREAM
- 1/3 CUP OIL
- 1/3 CUP WATER
- 4 EGGS
- 1 1/2 TEASPOONS CINNAMON
- 1/8 TEASPOON GINGER
- 1/8 TEASPOON ALLSPICE

FILLING

- 1 1/2 CUPS PEELED, CHOPPED APPLES
- 1/3 CUP FIRMLY PACKED BROWN SUGAR
- 1 TABLESPOON FLOUR
- 1/4 TEASPOON CINNAMON
- 2 TABLESPOONS BUTTER OR MARGARINE
- 1/2 CUP FINELY CHOPPED PECANS, TOASTED

FROSTING

- 1 (8-OUNCE) CAN CRUSHED PINEAPPLE, UNDRAINED
- 1 (4-SERVING) PACKAGE VANILLA INSTANT PUDDING MIX
- 1 (8-OUNCE) CONTAINER FROZEN WHIPPED TOPPING (REGULAR OR LITE), THAWED
- 1/2 CUP FINELY CHOPPED PECANS, TOASTED
  CINNAMON

Grease and flour 12-cup tube pan. In large bowl, combine all cake ingredients. Beat at medium speed just until blended, about 2 minutes. Spread batter in prepared pan.

Bake at 350° for 50 to 60 minutes or until toothpick inserted in center of cake comes out clean. Cool in pan for 15 minutes. Remove from pan to wire rack; cool completely. Place cake on serving plate.

In large saucepan, combine all filling ingredients except pecans. Cook over medium heat, stirring constantly, for 3 to 4 minutes or until apples are tender. Stir in nuts.

Mark center of side of cake with toothpicks. Using a long serrated knife, slice cake in half. Carefully remove top half. Spoon filling onto bottom half; replace top half.

For frosting, combine pineapple and pudding mix. Stir in whipped topping. Frost sides, top and center of cake. Sprinkle top with pecans; lightly sprinkle with cinnamon. Refrigerate until ready to use.

Note: To toast pecans, bake on 15x10-inch jelly roll pan at 325° for 8 to 10 minutes or until lightly browned, stirring once.

Dan Hastings
Plant Manager
Smucker Quality Beverages
Havre de Grace, Maryland
Employee since 1982

"This cake would be ideal on a cool night in front of a fire. Whatever the occasion, it's a pleaser!"

Creamy Fruit Blintzes

16 blintzes; 8 servings

CHEESE FILLING

- 1 EGG YOLK
- 2 TABLESPOONS SUGAR
- 1 (8-OUNCE) PACKAGE CREAM CHEESE, SOFTENED
- 2 CUPS (12-OUNCE CARTON) DRY OR CREAMED COTTAGE CHEESE
- ¼ TEASPOON VANILLA

BLINTZES

- 3 EGGS
- 3 TABLESPOONS OIL
- 1½ CUPS MILK
- 1 CUP ALL-PURPOSE FLOUR
- ½ TEASPOON SALT
- ⅓ CUP BUTTER OR MARGARINE, MELTED
- 2 TABLESPOONS BUTTER OR MARGARINE (UNMELTED)
- POWDERED SUGAR
- 1 CUP SOUR CREAM
- 1 CUP (12-OUNCE JAR) **SMUCKER'S** STRAWBERRY, CHERRY OR BLUEBERRY PRESERVES

Combine egg yolk and sugar; beat with electric mixer until thick and yellow. Add cream cheese, cottage cheese and vanilla; mix well. Refrigerate until ready to use.

Combine eggs, oil and milk; beat with electric mixer until well blended. Add flour and salt; continue to beat until batter is smooth and flour is dissolved. Refrigerate, covered, for 30 minutes or until ready to use.

Slowly heat small skillet. To test temperature, drop a little cold water onto surface; water should bead up and bounce. For each blintz, brush pan lightly with melted butter. Measure 3 tablespoons of batter into cup. Pour in all at once, rotating skillet quickly to spread evenly. Cook for 1 minute until golden brown on underside; loosen edge with spatula and remove. Dry on paper towels. Stack, brown side up, with waxed paper between blitzes.

Spread 3 tablespoons of filling on browned side of each blintz, making a rectangle 4 inches long. Fold two sides in over filling, overlapping edges and covering filling completely. Melt 1 tablespoon butter in large skillet over medium heat. Add half of blintzes, seam-side-down and not touching. Sauté until golden brown, turning once. Keep warm in low oven while cooking second half of blintzes. Serve hot, sprinkled with powdered sugar and topped with sour cream and preserves.

Note: As pictured, all four sides of blintzes may be folded in, overlapping edges to form a square. Filling is completely enclosed.

CREAMY FRUIT BLINTZES

Chocolate Peanut Butter Fudge

60 bars

½ CUP BUTTER OR MARGARINE, MELTED

1 ½ CUPS **SMUCKER'S** CREAMY NATURAL PEANUT BUTTER OR **LAURA SCUDDER'S** SMOOTH OLD-FASHIONED PEANUT BUTTER

3 CUPS POWDERED SUGAR

½ CUP FIRMLY PACKED BROWN SUGAR

1 ½ TEASPOONS VANILLA

1 CUP (6 OUNCES) SEMI-SWEET CHOCOLATE CHIPS

⅓ CUP BUTTER OR MARGARINE

Combine ½ cup butter, peanut butter, powdered sugar, brown sugar and vanilla; mix well. Press mixture into 13x9-inch pan.

Melt chocolate chips and ⅓ cup butter. Spread over peanut butter mixture. Refrigerate until firm. Cut into 1-inch squares.

Peanut Crumb Apple Pie

6 to 8 servings

1 CUP ALL-PURPOSE FLOUR

½ CUP **SMUCKER'S** CREAMY NATURAL PEANUT BUTTER OR **LAURA SCUDDER'S** SMOOTH OLD-FASHIONED PEANUT BUTTER

½ CUP FIRMLY PACKED LIGHT BROWN SUGAR

¼ CUP BUTTER OR MARGARINE, SOFTENED

¼ TEASPOON SALT

1 CAN (30-OUNCE) APPLE PIE FILLING

1 (9-INCH) UNBAKED PIE SHELL

Blend flour, peanut butter, brown sugar, butter and salt until mixture is crumbly. Spoon apple pie filling into unbaked crust; sprinkle peanut butter mixture over pie filling.

Bake at 400° for 30 to 35 minutes or until filling is hot and pastry is browned.

Brownie Pie à la Mode

8 servings

1 PINT VANILLA ICE CREAM,
  SLIGHTLY SOFTENED
1 (15 1/2-OUNCE) PACKAGE
  BROWNIE MIX
1/2 CUP CHOPPED WALNUTS
1/2 CUP **SMUCKER'S** CHOCOLATE
  FUDGE TOPPING
2 TABLESPOONS FLAKED COCONUT

Spoon ice cream into chilled 2-cup bowl or mold, packing it firmly with back of spoon. Cover with plastic wrap or aluminum foil; freeze at least 1 hour or until firm.

Prepare brownie mix according to package directions; stir in walnuts. Pour into greased 9-inch pie plate. Bake as directed on package. Cool completely on wire rack.

To serve, remove ice cream from freezer. Dip bowl in lukewarm water for 5 seconds. Cut around edge of ice cream with knife and invert onto center of brownie pie. Pour fudge topping over ice cream; sprinkle with coconut. Let stand 5 to 10 minutes at room temperature for easier slicing.

Caramel-Pecan Pie

6 to 8 servings

3 EGGS
2/3 CUP SUGAR
1 CUP (12-OUNCE JAR) **SMUCKER'S**
  CARAMEL TOPPING
1/4 CUP BUTTER OR MARGARINE,
  MELTED
1 1/2 CUPS PECAN HALVES
1 (9-INCH) UNBAKED PIE SHELL

In mixing bowl, beat eggs slightly with fork. Add sugar, stirring until dissolved. Stir in topping and butter; mix well. Stir in pecan halves. Pour filling into pie shell.

Bake at 350° for 45 minutes or until knife inserted near center comes out clean. Cool thoroughly on rack before serving. Cover, and store in refrigerator.

Spiced Apricot Pastries

5 dozen pastries

1 CUP (12-OUNCE JAR) **SMUCKER'S** APRICOT OR PEACH PRESERVES
½ CUP FINELY CHOPPED WALNUTS
¾ TEASPOON PUMPKIN PIE SPICE
½ TEASPOON GRATED ORANGE PEEL
1 CUP BUTTER OR MARGARINE, SOFTENED
1 (8-OUNCE) PACKAGE CREAM CHEESE, SOFTENED
2 TABLESPOONS SUGAR
½ TEASPOON VANILLA
2 CUPS ALL-PURPOSE FLOUR
1 EGG
1 TABLESPOON WATER
SIFTED POWDERED SUGAR

Combine preserves, walnuts, pumpkin pie spice and orange peel; mix well.

Beat butter, cream cheese, sugar and vanilla at medium speed until creamy. Add flour; beat at low speed until well blended.

Divide dough into thirds. On lightly floured surface, roll out each portion of dough to ⅛-inch thickness. Cut with 3-inch round cookie cutter.

Spoon ½ teaspoon apricot filling in center of each round. Combine egg and water; brush on edges. Fold opposite sides to center, slightly overlapping edges; pinch to seal. Place on lightly greased baking sheets.

Bake at 375° for 10 to 14 minutes or until light golden brown. Transfer to wire racks to cool. Sprinkle with powdered sugar.

SPICED APRICOT PASTRIES

Sweet Potato Meringue Pie

10 servings

1 (9-INCH) GRAHAM CRACKER CRUST

FILLING

2 WHOLE SWEET POTATOES OR
  1 (29-OUNCE) CAN SWEET
  POTATOES, DRAINED
1 CUP (12-OUNCE JAR) **SMUCKER'S**
  SWEET ORANGE MARMALADE
2 EGG YOLKS
¼ TEASPOON CINNAMON
¼ TEASPOON GINGER
⅛ TEASPOON ALLSPICE
⅛ TEASPOON NUTMEG
  PINCH OF SALT
1 CUP EVAPORATED SKIM MILK
3 TABLESPOONS CORNSTARCH

MERINGUE

3 EGG WHITES
  PINCH OF SALT
⅓ CUP SUGAR

Bake graham cracker crust at 400° for 10 minutes.

Meanwhile, pierce sweet potatoes with fork and microwave on High for 4 minutes. Combine sweet potatoes, marmalade, egg yolks, cinnamon, ginger, allspice, nutmeg and salt; stir to blend thoroughly. Stir in evaporated milk. Add cornstarch and stir until smooth.

Pour filling into pie crust. Bake at 400° for 45 to 55 minutes or until a knife inserted in the center comes out clean. Remove pie from oven and set aside to cool. Reduce oven heat to 350°.

Beat egg whites and salt with electric mixer until soft peaks form. Gradually add sugar; beat until egg whites are stiff and shiny. Carefully spread meringue over top of cooled pie. Bake at 350° for 15 minutes or until meringue is golden brown.

Cool pie on wire rack. Serve at room temperature or refrigerate and serve cold.

Peanut Butter Oatmeal Treats

3½ dozen cookies

1¾ CUPS ALL-PURPOSE FLOUR
 1 TEASPOON BAKING SODA
½ TEASPOON SALT
½ CUP BUTTER OR MARGARINE,
  SOFTENED
½ CUP **SMUCKER'S** CREAMY
  NATURAL PEANUT BUTTER
  OR **LAURA SCUDDER'S**
  SMOOTH OLD-FASHIONED
  PEANUT BUTTER
 1 CUP SUGAR
 1 CUP FIRMLY-PACKED
  LIGHT BROWN SUGAR
 2 EGGS
¼ CUP MILK
 1 TEASPOON VANILLA
2½ CUPS UNCOOKED OATS
 1 CUP SEMI-SWEET CHOCOLATE CHIPS

Combine flour, baking soda and salt; set aside. In large mixing bowl, combine butter, peanut butter, sugar and brown sugar. Beat until light and creamy. Beat in eggs, milk and vanilla. Stir in flour mixture, oats and chocolate chips. Drop dough by rounded teaspoonfuls about 3 inches apart onto ungreased cookie sheets.

Bake at 350° for 15 minutes or until lightly browned.

Southern Jam Cake

12 to 16 servings

CAKE

- 3/4 CUP BUTTER OR MARGARINE, SOFTENED
- 1 CUP SUGAR
- 3 EGGS
- 1 CUP (12-OUNCE JAR) **SMUCKER'S** SEEDLESS BLACKBERRY JAM
- 2 1/2 CUPS ALL-PURPOSE FLOUR
- 1 TEASPOON GROUND CINNAMON
- 1 TEASPOON GROUND CLOVES
- 1 TEASPOON GROUND ALLSPICE
- 1 TEASPOON GROUND NUTMEG
- 1 TEASPOON BAKING SODA
- 3/4 CUP BUTTERMILK

CARAMEL ICING, IF DESIRED

- 2 TABLESPOONS BUTTER
- 1/2 CUP FIRMLY PACKED BROWN SUGAR
- 3 TABLESPOONS MILK
- 1 3/4 CUPS POWDERED SUGAR

Grease and flour tube pan. Combine 3/4 cup butter and sugar; beat until light and fluffy. Add eggs one at a time, beating well after each addition. Fold in jam.

Combine flour, cinnamon, cloves, allspice, nutmeg and baking soda; mix well. Add to batter alternately with buttermilk, stirring just enough to blend after each addition. Spoon mixture into prepared pan.

Bake at 350° for 50 minutes or until toothpick inserted in center comes out clean. Cool in pan for 10 minutes. Remove from pan; cool completely.

In saucepan, melt 2 tablespoons butter; stir in brown sugar. Cook, stirring constantly, until mixture boils; remove from heat. Cool 5 minutes. Stir in milk; blend in powdered sugar. Frost cake.

Buttery Black Raspberry Bars

32 bars

- 1 CUP BUTTER OR MARGARINE
- 1 CUP SUGAR
- 2 EGG YOLKS
- 2 CUPS ALL-PURPOSE FLOUR
- 1 CUP CHOPPED WALNUTS
- 1/2 CUP **SMUCKER'S** SEEDLESS BLACK RASPBERRY JAM

Beat butter until soft and creamy. Gradually add sugar, beating until mixture is light and fluffy. Add egg yolks; blend well. Gradually add flour; mix thoroughly. Fold in walnuts.

Spoon half of batter into greased 8-inch square pan; spread evenly. Top with jam; cover with remaining batter.

Bake at 325° for 1 hour or until lightly browned. Cool and cut into 2x1-inch bars.

Orange Marmalade Cookies

5 dozen cookies

COOKIES

 2 CUPS SUGAR

½ CUP SHORTENING

 2 EGGS

 1 CUP SOUR CREAM

1/2 CUP **SMUCKER'S** SWEET ORANGE
   MARMALADE

 4 CUPS ALL-PURPOSE FLOUR

 2 TEASPOONS BAKING POWDER

 1 TEASPOON BAKING SODA

½ TEASPOON SALT

ICING

 3 CUPS POWDERED SUGAR

½ CUP BUTTER OR MARGARINE

¼ CUP **SMUCKER'S** SWEET ORANGE
   MARMALADE

   ORANGE JUICE

Combine sugar, shortening and eggs; beat until
well mixed. Add sour cream and ½ cup
marmalade; mix well. Add remaining cookie
ingredients; mix well. Chill dough.

Drop by rounded teaspoonfuls onto greased
cookie sheets. Bake at 400° for 8 to 10
minutes. Cool.

Combine all icing ingredients, adding enough
orange juice for desired spreading consistency
(none may be needed). Ice cooled cookies.

ORANGE MARMALADE COOKIES, CHEWY RED RASPBERRY BARS PAGE 92

Fruit Pizza

9 servings

1 (1 LB. 4-OUNCE) PACKAGE
   REFRIGERATED SUGAR COOKIE
   DOUGH
1 (8-OUNCE) PACKAGE
   CREAM CHEESE, SOFTENED
1 CUP POWDERED SUGAR
   ASSORTED FRESH FRUIT
   (STRAWBERRIES, BANANAS, KIWI
   FRUIT, BLUEBERRIES, MANDARIN
   ORANGES, ETC.)
½ CUP **SMUCKER'S** APRICOT
   PRESERVES OR SWEET ORANGE
   MARMALADE
1 TABLESPOON WATER

Cut dough into 1-inch slices and place on
ungreased cookie sheet or pizza pan. Bake
17 to 19 minutes or until light golden brown
around edges. Cool.

Combine cream cheese and sugar; mix well.
Spread over cookies. Decorate with sliced fruit.
(Dip banana slices in lemon juice to prevent
browning.) Combine preserves and water; mix
well. Drizzle over fruit topping. Serve
immediately or refrigerate until serving time.

Chocolate Icebox Cake

8 to 10 servings

18 LADYFINGERS, SPLIT
1 ENVELOPE UNFLAVORED GELATIN
2 TABLESPOONS SUGAR
¼ TEASPOON SALT
2 EGGS, SEPARATED
1 CUP MILK
1 CUP (12-OUNCE JAR) **SMUCKER'S** CHOCOLATE FUDGE TOPPING
½ TEASPOON VANILLA
1 CUP HEAVY OR WHIPPING CREAM, WHIPPED

Line 9x5-inch loaf pan with 2 crossed strips of waxed paper, extending paper beyond rim. Line bottom and sides with ladyfinger halves, cut sides up; set aside.

In medium saucepan, mix gelatin, 1 tablespoon of the sugar and salt. Beat together egg yolks, milk and fudge topping; stir into gelatin mixture.

Cook over low heat, stirring constantly, until gelatin dissolves, about 6 to 8 minutes. Remove from heat; stir in vanilla. Chill, stirring occasionally, until mixture mounds slightly when dropped from a spoon.

Beat egg whites until stiff but not dry; add remaining 1 tablespoon sugar and beat until very stiff. Fold ¼ of egg whites into chocolate mixture, then gently fold in whipped cream and remaining egg whites. Pour half of mixture into prepared pan; add layer of 9 ladyfinger halves, then remaining chocolate mixture. Top with remaining 9 ladyfinger halves, cut side down. Chill until firm, at least 4 hours or overnight.

To serve, using waxed paper, lift cake from pan and transfer to serving plate; gently remove waxed paper. Garnish top with additional chocolate fudge topping, if desired.

Note: For Chocolate Fudge Pie, substitute one 9-inch baked pastry or crumb crust for ladyfingers. Pour chocolate mixture into prepared pie shell. Chill until firm. Garnish with additional whipped cream and chocolate fudge topping.

Peanut Butter Cream Pie

8 servings

PECAN CRUST

1 1/2 CUPS FINELY CHOPPED PECANS, TOASTED

1/2 CUP SUGAR

1/4 CUP BUTTER OR MARGARINE, MELTED

1/4 TEASPOON CINNAMON

1/8 TEASPOON NUTMEG

FILLING

1 (8-OUNCE) PACKAGE CREAM CHEESE, SOFTENED

1 CUP **SMUCKER'S** CREAMY NATURAL PEANUT BUTTER OR **LAURA SCUDDER'S** SMOOTH OLD-FASHIONED PEANUT BUTTER

1 CUP POWDERED SUGAR

2 TABLESPOONS BUTTER OR MARGARINE, SOFTENED

2 1/2 CUPS FROZEN WHIPPED TOPPING, THAWED

3/4 CUP **SMUCKER'S** HOT FUDGE TOPPING

2 TABLESPOONS FINELY CHOPPED PECANS, TOASTED

Mix all crust ingredients in 9-inch metal pie pan; press onto bottom and up sides. Refrigerate crust until ready to use.

Combine cream cheese, peanut butter, powdered sugar and butter in large bowl; beat until fluffy. Fold in 1 cup whipped topping. (Refrigerate remaining whipped topping.) Spoon into crust. Cover and refrigerate until firm, about 2 hours.

Heat topping according to directions, spread fudge topping over pie, leaving 1-inch border. Spoon remaining 1½ cups whipped topping around border. Sprinkle with 2 tablespoons toasted pecans. Refrigerate at least 1 hour before serving.

Note: To toast pecans, bake on 15x10-inch jelly roll pan at 325° for 8 to 10 minutes or until lightly browned, stirring once.

Marbled Peanut Butter Brownies

24 bars

2/3 CUP ALL-PURPOSE OR WHOLE-WHEAT FLOUR

1/2 TEASPOON BAKING POWDER

1/4 TEASPOON SALT

1/2 CUP **SMUCKER'S** CREAMY NATURAL PEANUT BUTTER OR **LAURA SCUDDER'S** SMOOTH OLD-FASHIONED PEANUT BUTTER

1/4 CUP BUTTER OR MARGARINE, SOFTENED

3/4 CUP FIRMLY PACKED BROWN SUGAR

2 EGGS

1 TEASPOON VANILLA

3 (1-OUNCE) SQUARES SEMI-SWEET CHOCOLATE OR 1/2 CUP SEMI-SWEET CHOCOLATE CHIPS, MELTED AND COOLED

Combine flour, baking powder and salt; set aside.

In small bowl of mixer, combine peanut butter, butter and brown sugar; beat until light and creamy. Add eggs and vanilla; beat until fluffy. Stir in flour mixture just until blended. Spread in greased 8-inch square baking pan. Drizzle on chocolate, then with table knife swirl into batter to marble.

Bake at 350° for 25 to 30 minutes or until toothpick inserted in center comes out clean. Cool in pan on rack. Cut into 24 bars.

Chocolate Raspberry Cake

12 to 15 servings

- 4 (1-OUNCE) SQUARES UNSWEETENED CHOCOLATE
- 1/4 CUP WATER
- 1/2 CUP BUTTER OR MARGARINE, CUT INTO SMALL PIECES
- 1/2 CUP SUGAR
- 3 EGGS, SEPARATED
- 1/3 CUP UNSIFTED ALL-PURPOSE FLOUR
- 1/2 CUP **SMUCKER'S** RED RASPBERRY PRESERVES OR APRICOT PRESERVES
- CHOCOLATE SHAVINGS
- FRESH RASPBERRIES

Grease and flour two 8-inch round cake pans; set aside. In medium saucepan, melt chocolate and water over low heat, stirring constantly. Add butter; stir until completely melted. Remove from heat and blend in sugar; cool.

Add egg yolks, beating well after each addition. Add flour to chocolate mixture; blend well. Beat egg whites until stiff but not dry; fold into chocolate mixture. Pour into prepared cake pans.

Bake at 325° for about 25 minutes or until toothpick inserted into center of cake comes out clean.

Heat preserves in saucepan until melted. Spread half of preserves on 1 layer. Top with second layer; spread with remaining preserves. Garnish with chocolate shavings and raspberries.

Note: For chocolate shavings, melt 1 to 2 ounces of semi-sweet chocolate. Spread melted chocolate in thin layer on cookie sheet; refrigerate until set. Scrape with metal spatula held at 45° angle to produce shavings and curls. Chill or freeze shavings until ready to use.

CHOCOLATE RASPBERRY CAKE

Orange Peanut Butter Bars

16 bars

BARS

- 1 ½ CUPS ALL-PURPOSE FLOUR
- ½ TEASPOON BAKING SODA
- ½ TEASPOON SALT
- ½ CUP BUTTER OR MARGARINE
- ½ CUP SUGAR
- ½ CUP FIRMLY PACKED LIGHT BROWN SUGAR
- ½ CUP **SMUCKER'S** CREAMY NATURAL PEANUT BUTTER OR **LAURA SCUDDER'S** SMOOTH OLD-FASHIONED PEANUT BUTTER
- 1 EGG
- ¼ CUP MILK
- ½ TEASPOON VANILLA

ORANGE FROSTING

- 2 CUPS POWDERED SUGAR
- ¼ CUP **SMUCKER'S** SWEET ORANGE MARMALADE
- 2 TO 3 TEASPOONS MILK

CHOCOLATE ICING

- ½ SQUARE (½-OUNCE) UNSWEETENED CHOCOLATE
- ¼ TEASPOON SHORTENING

Combine flour, baking soda and salt; set aside. In medium saucepan, melt butter over moderate heat. Remove pan from heat. Add sugar, brown sugar and peanut butter; beat with wooden spoon until thoroughly mixed. Blend in egg, milk and vanilla until thick. Stir in flour mixture until well blended. Spread in greased 9-inch square pan.

Bake at 375° for 25 minutes, or until top springs back when lightly touched. Cool completely.

Mix powdered sugar and marmalade until evenly blended. Gradually add enough milk for desired spreading consistency. Spread frosting over bars.

In a small bowl, melt chocolate and shortening over boiling water. Drizzle chocolate icing across frosting in lines about 1 inch apart. Cut into bars.

Elegant Berry Trifle

10 to 12 servings

- 3 (3-OUNCE) PACKAGES VANILLA PUDDING MIX
- 6 CUPS MILK
- 1 ½ TEASPOONS ALMOND EXTRACT
- ½ CUP WHITE GRAPE JUICE
- 1 (12-OUNCE) LOAF POUND CAKE, CUT INTO ½-INCH SLICES
- ½ CUP **SMUCKER'S** RED RASPBERRY PRESERVES
- ½ CUP **SMUCKER'S** BLACKBERRY PRESERVES
- 1 CUP WHIPPING CREAM
- 1 TABLESPOON POWDERED SUGAR
- 1 TEASPOON VANILLA
- 8 CRISP ALMOND MACAROON COOKIES, CRUSHED, OR ¼ CUP TOASTED SLIVERED ALMONDS

Prepare pudding mixes according to package directions; cool. Blend in 1 teaspoon of the almond extract. Combine remaining ½ teaspoon extract with grape juice. Set aside.

Spread ¼ of pound cake slices with raspberry preserves and ¼ with blackberry preserves; top each spread slice with unspread slice to form "sandwiches". Cut sandwiches into ¾-inch-wide pieces. Reserve a few to garnish top of trifle; sprinkle remaining pieces with grape juice mixture.

To assemble trifle, spoon ⅓ of pudding into 6-cup dessert dish or trifle bowl. Alternate raspberry and blackberry cake pieces in pattern on pudding, using half of pieces. Repeat procedure. Top with remaining pudding. Chill several hours.

Shortly before serving, whip cream with powdered sugar and vanilla until soft peaks form. Sprinkle crushed macaroons around edge of dish. Pipe rosettes or spoon dollops of whipped cream on top of trifle; garnish with reserved cake pieces.